Almond Flour! Gluten Free & Paleo Diet Cookbook

47 Irresistible Cooking & Baking Recipes for Wheat Free, Paleo and Celiac Diets (Gluten-Free Goodness Series)

Donatella Giordano

Atlanta, Georgia USA

ISBN 978-1-48396-897-1

All Rights Reserved

No part of this book may be reproduced or transmitted for resale or use by any party other than the individual purchaser who is the sole authorized user of this information. Purchaser is authorized to use any of the information in this publication for his or her own use only. All other reproduction or transmission, or any form or by any means, electronic or mechanical, including photocopying, recording or by any informational storage or retrieval system, is prohibited without express written permission from the author.

Copyright © 2012 Donatella Giordano

What Our Readers Are Saying

"This book gave me more than I bargained for; a real treasure-trove of delicious recipes."

★★★★☆ **Christina D. Acosta (Oakfield, ME)**

"I've been on a gluten free diet for quite some time now, but thanks to books like this I've been able to enjoy eating and cooking just as much as I used to in the past."

★★★★★ **Kate W. Georges (Woodbridge, NJ)**

"I never thought that following a specific diet could be so fun and creative at the same time. These recipes are easy to make and as tasty as they come."

★★★★★ **Tania O. McBride (Mary Alice, KY)**

Exclusive Bonus Download: Coconut Oil - The Healthy Fat

Coconut oil the complete natural health guide!

Find out the health benefits of coconut oil today!

Find out how coconut oil can, cure common illnesses saving you hundreds in doctors' fees, help you lose weight without losing the great taste of your favorite foods and much, much more!

Coconut oil has long been held in high repute by natural health specialists and doctors from a massively diverse range of countries. Western medicine has been slow to catch on to the health benefits of coconut oil but cutting edge research is finally catching up to what eastern doctors have known for centuries; COCONUT OIL IS GOOD FOR YOU!

Whilst many claims are made about the benefits of coconut oil in your diet and as a topical skin treatment finding good information on the wide range of benefits coconut oil can have for you can be incredibly time consuming and tricky.

Get the Facts about coconut oil health today!

This eBook has been compiled for exactly these reasons we have spent weeks crawling cyberspace and reading medical reports to try and find as much concrete information on the myriad of benefits that coconut oil can offer YOU. This guide gives you a complete breakdown of all the health benefits of coconut oil and a complete guide to how YOU can start using it to improve your health.

This book tells you when to use coconut oil, why you should be using coconut oil and how coconut oil can improve your health AND cure common illnesses

Our complete guide to natural coconut oil health gives you a comprehensive insight into:

- Coconut oil and your hair – Find out whether coconut oil can improve the condition of your hair. Plus a comprehensive exposition of whether coconut oil can prevent hair loss and re-invigorate your hair.
- Coconut oil and skincare – Find out how coconut oil can keep your skin looking young fresh and firm. Plus find out which skin afflictions and disease you can cure just with coconut oil!
- Coconut oil and weight loss – Find out why coconut oil is a surprisingly effective aid to weight loss and how best to get it into your diet. Learn how you can utilize coconut oil and start shedding pounds now!
- Coconut oil and digestion – Find out how coconut oil can cure indigestion, how coconut oils help your digestive system stay healthy and why coconut oil increases your metabolism.
- Coconut oil and your immune system – Find out how coconut oil can drastically improve your immune system as part of a well-balanced diet.
- Can coconut oil help fight infections? – Find out about the huge number of infections simple, natural coconut oil can fight and how it can prevent common illnesses.
- And finally
- Coconut oil and heart disease – Find out the truth about one of the most controversial claims being made NOW about coconut oil. We examine the evidence in depth and see what the benefits are of coconut oil for a healthy heart.

This book covers everything you could ever need to know about coconut oil and will save you hundreds of dollars on expensive medicines and beauty products.

Knowing the secrets we reveal in this book will improve your health and will be an important step in helping you to live a long and fruitful life. Happy health!

<u>Download this guide and start overall health and weight loss goals NOW</u>

Thank you for downloading my book. Please REVIEW this book on Amazon. I need your feedback to make the next version better. Thank you so much!

Books by Donatella Giordano

Coconut Flour! 47+ Irresistible Recipes for Baking with Coconut Flour

Almond Flour! Gluten Free & Paleo Diet Cookbook

www.amazon.com/author/donatellagiordano

Why You Should Read This Book?

I've always been passionate about cooking so it came as no surprise that I ended up becoming a chef and then an author of cookbooks. What you eat is very important, and I for one know that for sure. So, I believe that one should share her cooking experiences with the others in order to make the world a better place. I know that that sounds a bit presumptuous but that doesn't mean it's not true. If you've studied a bit of history you'll know that a lot of treaties have been signed around a dinner table, and a lot deals have been reached over a meal as well.

"Why write a cookbook with almond flour recipes?" you may be wondering. The short answer is: Because almond flour is good for your health. As someone who've spent a lifetime cooking and researching food, allow me to say that almond flour can give you what wheat flour can't: Extra nutrients, a gateway to a different and healthier diet, and last but not least, a great taste.

If you buy this book you'll find yourself in a new culinary adventure that's not only interesting and delicious but also fun. Creating these recipes was a joy; a joy that I now wish to share with you.

TABLE OF CONTENTS

ALL YOU NEED TO KNOW ABOUT ALMOND FLOUR 13

IT'S ALL ABOUT ALMONDS 15
Nutritional and health benefits of eating almonds 15

THE BENEFITS OF USING ALMOND FLOUR 17
Gluten sensitivity symptoms include 17
Almond flour versus other gluten-free alternatives 17

ALMOND FLOUR IN THE PALEO DIET 21

ALMOND FLOUR IN THE RAW FOOD DIET 23

WHERE TO BUY ALMOND FLOUR 25

MAKING YOUR OWN ALMOND FLOUR 27
Natural almonds versus flavored almonds 28
Making almond flour from almond milk pulp 28
Buying almonds to make your own almond flour 28

STORING ALMONDS 31

STORING ALMOND FLOUR 33

SUBSTITUTING ALMOND FLOUR IN RECIPES 35

IN CONCLUSION 37

SOUPS 39
1. Almond and Grape Cream with Aromatic Oil 39

Peppermint oil: 40

2. Fresh Apple Cream with Almond Flour and Zucchini 40

3. Almond and Saffron Soup 41

4. Warm Broccoli and Almond Soup 42

VEGETARIAN 45

5. Almond Flour Bread 45

6. Savory Crackers 46

7. Vegetarian Loaf 47

8. "Breaded" Tomatoes 49

9. Paleo Buns 50

10. Vegetarian Lasagna 51

11. Zucchini Noodles with Almond and Basil Pesto Sauce 52

FISH 55

12. Paleo Fish Cakes 55

13. Perch Fillet with Coconut Milk Sauce 56

14. Salmon with Black Olive and Almond Crust 57

15. Oven Baked Cod 58

16. Mediterranean Swordfish Steaks 60

MEAT 63

17. Spiced Muffins 63

18. Beef Medallion with an Herb Crust 64

19. Ham and Spinach Stuffed Chicken Breasts 66

20. Veal Scallops with Creamy Almond Sauce 67

21. Low-carb Turkey Meatballs 69

22. Bacon Quiche 71

23. Home-made Hamburger 72

DESSERTS, CAKES, MUFFINS, AND OTHER SWEET TREATS 75

24. Orange Cake 75

25. Surprise Muffins 76

26. Chocolate Brownies 77

27. Apple Crunch 78

28. Fake Chocolate Truffles 79

29. Spicy Chocolate Cake 80

30. Peanut Cookies 81

31. Almond Biscuits 82

32. Coffee and Vanilla Delights 83

33. Crust-less Fresh Plum Pie 84

34. Dried Apricot and Strawberry Cake 85

35. Pancakes 86

36. Fig and Almond Ice Cream 87

37. Baked Pears with Almond Crust 88

38. Almond Meringues 89

39. Panforte 90

40. Banana Muffins 91

41. Nuts and Dates No-Bake Brownie 92

42. Almond Mousse 93

43. Crusted Apple Pie 94

44. Raspberry and Blueberry Bars 96

45. Chocolate and Coconut Biscuits 97

46. Almond and Flaxseed Muffins 98

47. Orange and Apricot Muffins 99

EXCLUSIVE BONUS DOWNLOAD: COCONUT OIL - THE HEALTHY FAT 100

ONE LAST THING... 102

Disclaimer

While all attempts have been made to provide effective, verifiable information in this Book, neither the Author nor Publisher assumes any responsibility for errors, inaccuracies, or omissions. Any slights of people or organizations are unintentional.

This Book is not a source of medical information, and it should not be regarded as such. This publication is designed to provide accurate and authoritative information in regard to the subject matter covered. It is sold with the understanding that the publisher is not engaged in rendering a medical service. As with any medical advice, the reader is strongly encouraged to seek professional medical advice before taking action.

All You Need to Know About Almond Flour

With a growing number of people beginning to realize the benefits of exchanging a diet of highly processed sugary foods for a diet of fresh foods and foods that are much closer to their natural state, almond flour provides a gluten-free alternative to wheat flour that is low in carbohydrate and low in sugar but high in protein and packed with health-boosting nutrients. It's made by simply grinding whole almonds to the desired consistency and no other ingredients are added, making it a "super food" that's suitable for those choosing a Paleo-style diet or raw food diet, or anyone interested in giving their body a helping-hand through the inclusion of more healthful natural foods in their daily diet. Almond flour can be used as a substitute for regular flour in a wide variety of ways, and anecdotal evidence suggests it comes out on top when compared to other gluten-free flour alternatives in terms of ease of use as well as taste in cooking and baking.

It's All About Almonds

We commonly refer to almonds as nuts but they are in fact the seeds of the fruit produced by almond trees. The fruit is known as a drupe and has a hard outer shell containing the almond "nut" inside. Packaged almonds, normally without their shells, can be found in stores all over the world throughout the year but the peak season for sourcing fresh almonds is mid-summer. The almond tree thrives in the warm climate of the Mediterranean with many grown in Spain, Morocco, Portugal and Italy, but it's California in the US that currently produces the largest amount of commercially grown almonds, providing around 80 percent of the world's supplies. According to the Food and Agriculture Organization, the world currently produces over 2.5 million tons of almonds each year.

Nutritional and health benefits of eating almonds

- **Almonds can lower LDL cholesterol**

Almonds have been medically proven to help lower LDL cholesterol and thereby reduce the risk of developing heart disease. LDL cholesterol is the "bad" form of cholesterol and high levels in your blood can lead to damage in the lining of your arteries and eventually increase the potential for blockages in your bloodstream; this is known as atherosclerosis.

- **Almonds can help protect against diabetes**

Studies have shown that almonds can help to minimize the rise of blood sugar levels at mealtimes. As a low GI food, almonds provide a slow release of energy, thereby reducing the potential for rapid sugar "spikes" to occur, and researchers have found that their presence in the diet can help to lower the GI of other foods being eaten. High levels of blood sugar are associated with the onset of diabetes and cardiovascular disease.

- **Almonds provide a rich source of vitamin E**

Vitamin E plays an important antioxidant role in your body. Antioxidants defend the cells in your body from the potentially damaging effects of free radicals – chemicals produced by the body which can be harmful if left unchecked. Research suggests that vitamin E may help to protect against heart disease and some forms of cancer.

Almonds are an excellent source of manganese

Manganese plays a vital role in energy production. It also helps to promote strong bone growth and is needed by the liver to store glucose.

- **Almonds are high in protein**

The high protein content of almonds makes them a particularly useful addition to a vegetarian diet. Almonds typically contain over 7 grams of protein, a higher value than an egg which typically contains just over 5 grams of protein. Protein is essential in the diet to promote healthy growth and repair of the cells in your body.

- **Almonds provide a useful source of magnesium, vitamin B2, copper and phosphorus**

Magnesium – this mineral promotes healthy bones and teeth, and is important for muscle contraction and healthy nerve impulses. Low levels of magnesium in the diet have been linked to an increased potential to suffer a heart attack.

Vitamin B2 – this vitamin is essential for the release of energy from food. It is also required to promote the proper functioning of vitamin B6 which is needed to release energy from proteins.

Copper – this mineral is needed to help the body absorb iron from food.

Phosphorus – this mineral is essential for the absorption of nutrients in the body.

- **Almonds can help to protect against high blood pressure**

Almonds are low in sodium and high in potassium; providing the optimal ratio to help maintain healthy blood pressure and a regular heartbeat.

- **Almonds can help overweight individuals to lose weight**

The results of a study published in the *International Journal of Obesity and Related Metabolic Disorders* show that a low calorie diet containing almonds proved more effective in shedding pounds than a low calorie diet containing complex carbohydrates. Almonds are high in fat but the biggest percentage is monounsaturated fat which is the "healthy" type of fat. Replacing unhealthy saturated fats with monounsaturated fats in the diet has been shown to lower cholesterol levels in the blood and according to the results of *The Nurses' Health Study*, replacing carbohydrates with nuts can lead to a 30 percent lowered risk of developing heart disease, and eating nuts in place of meat and dairy products can lead to a 45 percent reduction in risk.

The Benefits of Using Almond Flour

Almond flour is low in carbohydrate but high in protein and "healthy" monounsaturated fat. The fat content of a half cup is around 30 grams but only two of those grams are unhealthy saturated fat. A half cup also provides 14 grams of protein and only 10 grams of carbohydrate, half of which is dietary fiber, making it a versatile substitute for wheat flour for those on a low-carb diet. Consuming foods made with almond flour in your daily diet provides all of the health benefits listed above, making it a healthy, nutritious and gluten-free alternative to regular flour even when not on a carbohydrate restricted diet. For sufferers of celiac disease, eating a gluten-free diet is a necessity but for many others, removing foods containing wheat, barley and rye grain from the diet is a healthy-eating choice, helping to alleviate the commonly associated symptoms of gluten sensitivity or wheat intolerance.

Gluten sensitivity symptoms include

- Digestive upsets, including gas, abdominal cramps, bloating, diarrhea or constipation.
- Fatigue and feelings of "sleepiness" after meals.
- Sudden mood swings and irritability.
- Headaches
- Dizziness, sometimes accompanied by tingling sensations in the extremities.
- Weak or painful joints.

Almond flour is made from ground almonds which have had the skins removed (blanched almonds) and should not be confused with **almond meal**, which is made from ground almonds with the skins still intact. This means in terms of use in cooking and baking, the difference between the two can be likened to the difference between regular white flour and whole-meal flour, producing very different end results and therefore not always interchangeable in recipes. However, both almond flour and almond meal are gluten-free alternatives to wheat flour with the difference between the two being more noticeable in terms of end product texture as opposed to taste, although the flecks of skin still visible in almond meal produce a darker color and sometimes an earthier taste depending on the recipe.

Almond flour versus other gluten-free alternatives

One of the most readily available gluten-free flour alternatives is white rice flour. However, a common complaint with its usage is that the end results tend to have a sticky or gummy texture and a comparatively bland taste. Brown rice flour has a much nuttier flavor compared to white rice flour but there are health concerns associated with daily rice consumption and the Food and Drugs Administration in the US is currently investigating arsenic levels in rice. Other alternatives in popular use include the following:

- **Soybean flour** – this flour provides a bean-like flavor and works well in cookies and quick breads. However, it's not recommended for use on its own as substituting more than 40 percent of the overall flour content with soybean flour causes overly rapid browning during cooking.
- **Chick pea flour** – also known as **gram flour**, the earthy flavor provided by this flour makes it best suited to savory dishes and is most commonly used in Indian recipes.
- **Hazelnut flour** – compared to the subtle nutty flavor provided by almond flour, the taste of hazelnut flour can overpower other recipe ingredients.
- **Peanut flour** – as with hazelnut flour, the taste provided by peanut flour can be overpowering. Peanut allergies also make this product unsuitable for a growing number of people.
- **Coconut flour** – like almond flour, coconut flour provides a sweet flavor. However, this flour has a sponge-like effect during cooking which can lead to an overly dry end product as the moisture is soaked up.
- **Sorghum flour** – like soybean flour, this flour is not recommended for sole use in recipes as it produces a dry and slightly gritty textured end product. For this reason it is best used in a mix of other gluten-free flours.
- **Millet** – this flour provides a sweet flavor in recipes but also works best when blended into a mix of other gluten-free flours. However, there is controversy over its suitability for sufferers of hypothyroidism and it's currently recommended that individuals with the condition should consume no more than three servings per day.
- **Teff** – this flour is made from grass grains (the smallest grains in existence with the weight of 150 teff grains equaling the weight of just one wheat grain) and comes in white, brown and red varieties. The white variety has a mild nutty flavor but the darker grains pack an earthier punch which can be an acquired taste.
- **Buckwheat** – buckwheat grains are in fact not grains at all as buckwheat is a member of the rhubarb family. The flour is a greyish color and produces a slightly sour taste which can be overpowering. The nutty flavor given is much stronger than the subtle nutty flavor of almond flour.
- **Quinoa** – this is another "faux grain" which is actually a seed. Like teff, it comes in three different colored varieties but it has a fairly distinctive flavor and can therefore be an acquired taste. In baking, it's also best used as part of a gluten-free flour mix as quinoa flour used on its own tends to produce an overly crumbly end product.

Overall, according to online forums and gluten-free cookery book authors, almond flour is the preferred wheat flour alternative in most gluten-free baking recipes for both amateur and professional cooks, providing a moist, manageable consistency and adding just a subtle hint of nuttiness to the flavor. However, end products are generally much denser than wheat flour equivalents so a degree of trial and error and blending with other gluten-free flours may be needed to find the consistency you like.

Popular uses of almond flour include:

Baking – almond flour can be used in baking to make cakes and muffins, and also a variety of cookies.

Pancakes – almond flour mixes well with eggs and milk to make a delicious pancake batter.

Pastries – almond flour adds a delicate nutty flavor to pastry bases for use in sweet or savory dishes.

Bread – as it's gluten-free, almond flour is best suited to "quick breads" that don't require the dough to be kneaded, but with the addition of xanthan gum or a similar binding agent to replace the stickiness of the gluten present in wheat flour, a variety of breads can be made. Almond flour makes delicious pizza dough and it can also be used to make a wide variety of healthful crackers.

Thickening agent – almond flour provides a gluten-free and low calorie alternative to regular flour or cornstarch to thicken soups, stews, or gravy.

Smoothies – the addition of a spoonful of almond flour to a fruit or green smoothie helps to give a further boost to the nutritional value and can also add substance to give a "creamier" texture. Almond flour can also be sprinkled onto natural yogurt or ice-cream to give an added nutty taste that's packed with nutrients.

Salad dressing – in addition to adding to the nutritional value, almond flour in salad dressings gives a delicious nuttiness to the flavor without overpowering the other ingredients.

Almond Flour in the Paleo Diet

The Paleolithic diet, generally known as the Paleo diet, is the result of many years of research into the diet of our hunter-gatherer ancestors in the Paleolithic era (the time of our "caveman" ancestors from over 2 million years ago until the beginning of agriculture) by Dr. Loren Cordain. The diet is based on eating only foods from the food groups that would have been available to our Paleolithic ancestors.

Paleo foods include:

- **Fresh meat** – grass-fed or free-range beef, pork, lamb and poultry is preferable to grain-fed. Game such as venison, wild boar, rabbit, and pheasant is also Paleo if available.
- **Fish** – wild fish is preferable to farmed fish.
- **Seafood** – oysters, mussels, scallops, crabs, shrimp, clams.
- **Eggs**
- **Fresh fruits** – berries in particular.
- **Vegetables** – green leafy vegetables and cruciferous varieties especially, and excluding farmed vegetables such as carrots.
- **Tubers** – yams and sweet potatoes in particular.
- **Seeds and nuts** – excluding peanuts.
- **Healthy varieties of oil** – olive, coconut, avocado, macadamia, walnut and flaxseed.

In essence, a Paleo diet cuts all processed foods and refined sugars from your daily diet along with other foods that would not have been available in Paleolithic times such as dairy products, cereal grains and legumes. This means that foods made with wheat flour cannot be included in a Paleo diet but foods made with almond flour can. However, it must be noted that "Paleo purists" would choose not to include any type of baked "treat" foods such as cakes and muffins, even when made with almond flour and other ingredients that are technically "Paleo" as the whole ethos of the diet is to move away from the modern-day western culture of "eating for the sake of eating," and eating instead to provide the body with an optimal fuel source for health and vitality. But, with that said, there are still many benefits to be had from eating a Paleo-style diet – even with a few concessions now and then – and aiming to consume good quality organically grown produce, sourced locally whenever possible, is all part of cutting back on unhealthy processed foods and eating a diet that's closer to the food groups our ancestors lived and thrived on.

Dr. Loren Cordain believes that the prevalence of chronic illnesses and health issues in modern society is the result of moving away from a Paleolithic diet, and conditions such as cardiovascular disease – including heart disease, high blood pressure, and atherosclerosis – along with type II diabetes and cancer could be prevented by simply returning to a more natural diet and lifestyle.

Almond tree ancestry:

Interestingly, the ancient ancestors of the domesticated almond tree we know today are wild almond trees which produce a "nut" that has a bitter taste and is highly toxic if consumed. Originally native to Middle Eastern countries, historians believe that almond trees were one of the earliest trees to be domesticated and almond discoveries have been made in archeological sites in Jordan dating back to the early Bronze Age, some 2000+ years BC, and another significant find was made in Egypt in the tomb of Tutankhamun dating back to around 1325 BC. The ancient Egyptians are known to have used almonds, both the bitter toxic variety and the sweet edible variety, in many of their medicinal potions and although not yet scientifically proven, many people today believe that the powerful antioxidant properties of almonds may actually promote longevity as well as boost overall health and wellbeing.

Almond Flour in the Raw Food Diet

Almond flour is a staple ingredient in many raw food recipes. As the name suggests, a raw food diet consists of eating raw foods in their natural state with fruits and vegetables making up around 75 percent of the daily food intake.

Everyday staples include:

- Sprouts
- Sprouted seeds
- Seaweed
- Beans
- Whole grains
- Nuts
- Dried fruits

By eliminating refined sugars and toxins such as caffeine and alcohol, a "rawism" lifestyle provides a diet that's nutrient-dense, high in fiber and low in fat. Medical opinion is mixed on the benefits of eating uncooked foods but several studies have shown that a diet containing raw cruciferous vegetables can help to lower the risk of developing certain cancers.

In place of cooking, foods can be prepared using a food dehydrator to "heat" ingredients to temperatures of no more than 118 degrees F, thereby maintaining the digestive enzyme properties of the foods in their raw state; properties believed by raw food advocates to be destroyed by conventional cooking at high temperatures. Almond flour can be used to create nutrient-packed breads, pie crusts, pizza bases, and even a delicious variety of "raw" cakes and cookies.

Since 2007, all almonds produced commercially in the US must be pasteurized by law. This is due to a number of cases of food poisoning (salmonellosis) being connected to almond consumption. Packaged almonds labeled as "raw" and on sale in the US have actually been through a pasteurization process or chemical treatment and as such can no longer be considered a raw foodstuff in terms of adhering to a raw food diet. However, it is still possible to find truly raw almonds in their natural state as the law does not apply to almond growers who sell directly to the public in a small way.

Where to Buy Almond Flour

Almond flour and almond meal are generally available in health food stores. However, it can be expensive compared to regular flour at an average cost of anything from $7 per pound to around $12 per pound. For this reason, buying in bulk and buying online are popular choices as this helps to minimize the costs. Keying the words "almond flour" into a search engine will throw up a whole world (literally!) of choice in terms of brand and package weight options. Finding the best brand for you may once again require a process of trial-and-error and the best variety to use may vary from recipe to recipe. However, the most commonly available types of almond flour include the following:

Blanched almond flour – this is made from ground almonds that have had their skins removed. The skinning process generally involves some form of steaming to loosen the skins before their removal and the resulting blanched nuts are then dehydrated before grinding. Commercially produced blanched almond flour is generally the finest and lightest grind available.

Raw blanched almonds – this "raw" variety is prepared by soaking the almonds to soften and remove the skins before dehydrating and no heat processes are used. However, as all almonds grown commercially in the US are subjected to pasteurization by law, all almond flours and meals produced in the US are technically no longer truly raw, even though they may be labeled as such on the packaging. For those on a raw food diet, it's important to source products that have not been subjected to high heat at any point in the manufacturing process.

Almond meal – this is made from ground almonds with the skins left on. In many recipes, almond flour and almond meal are effectively interchangeable but almond meal tends to be a coarser grind and therefore not always suitable for cakes and baked goods that generally work best with a much finer grind.

To get the best results when cooking or baking with almond flour, it's always best to use the type and brand recommended and used by the creator of the recipe. This will help to ensure you get a similar end result but it doesn't mean that a little experimentation won't yield an even better result! The best product for you is the one that matches your dietary needs and preferences, and the best end result is really a matter of personal taste. Manufacturer's labels will provide the information you need to help you make the best choice. For example, you might need to check whether the contents are certified gluten-free; whether chemicals are used in the blanching process; whether the contents are organically grown, and whether the flour is a fine or a coarse grind. It's also worth noting that almond flour may be known by a different name in different parts of the world. In the UK for example, almond flour is packaged and labeled as "ground almonds" and in some other areas, almond flour may be packaged as almond meal even when the skins have been removed. For this reason, it's important to check the package contents list to make sure that you're getting exactly what you expect.

The almonds used in commercially produced blanched almond flour are not soaked before the skins are removed and some people find that this can lead to stomach and digestive upsets. Soaking almonds maximizes the release of the enzymes they contain, allowing your body to get the most out of them in terms of healthful nutrients, and it also makes them easier to digest. For this reason, many people are now choosing to make their own almond flour at home.

Making Your Own Almond Flour

If you have a food processor, blender, or electric coffee grinder at home, making your own almond flour is incredibly quick and easy.

- **Blanch the almonds** – remove the almond skins by steaming the almonds or boiling them in water for just a minute or two. This softens the skins and makes it very easy to remove them by simply rubbing your fingers and thumbs over them. If boiling, the almonds should be rinsed with cold water to stop the "cooking" process before removing the skins, and also to cool them before handling them!
- **Dry the blanched almonds** – once the skins are removed, the almonds must be dried as thoroughly as possible before grinding them. Excess water in the grinding process is likely to cause the flour to begin clumping together.
- **Process, blend, or grind** – place the dry, blanched almonds into a food processor, blender, or coffee grinder. With a high-speed blender it takes only 15 to 20 seconds of pulsing to produce a floury consistency, so care must be taken not to over-blend as the almonds will quickly turn to butter rather than flour. It can take slightly longer to achieve the desired floury consistency in a food processor and using the pulse setting is the best way to avoid the potential for heat to build up, causing the almonds to form a buttery consistency. In recipes that include sugar, adding a little of the sugar to the almonds as you grind them can help to keep the "grainy" consistency and limit the potential for them to turn to a paste. The same pulsing effect can be achieved when using an electric coffee grinder by simply switching it on and off in short bursts. In each case, grinding no more than a cupful of almonds at one time is preferable, limiting the potential for uneven grinding.
- **Sift the flour** – to get a finer grind without risking the flour turning to butter, sift the results of each 15 seconds or so of grinding through a flour sifter and return the lumps that are too big to sift through to the blender each time. This prevents over-grinding of the already finely ground almonds and creates a more evenly ground end result.

To make almond flour suitable for a raw food diet, raw almonds can be soaked overnight to soften the skins for easy removal and then dried in a food dehydrator before grinding. It's worth noting that the air temperature and humidity of the room will have a direct impact on the effectiveness of the food dehydrator and therefore the length of time needed to dry out the almonds. Some "rawism" followers choose to sprout the almonds before preparing them for grinding into flour. This process involves soaking the almonds in water overnight, rinsing them in fresh water, and then storing them in a lidded glass container in the refrigerator for one to three days until they sprout. Sprouted almonds are easier to digest and also softer, moister and sweeter in taste.

Natural almonds versus flavored almonds

The almonds used to make almond flour are almonds in their natural state with no other added ingredients or flavorings. One of the most popular ways to vary the flavor of almonds is to roast them but everything from butter toffee flavor to garlic flavor can also be found. Almond flour could be made from roasted almonds, especially dry roasted varieties, and the flour would retain the added flavor, but it would be best used straight away rather than stored. Other added flavorings tend to create an outer coating on the skin of the almond and this generally renders them unsuitable for grinding into flour as they are more likely to turn into an oily paste instead. Of course, if you like the idea of butter toffee or garlic flavors, there's no reason why you can't add them to your recipe in a different way.

Sugared almonds are also a popular, if not quite so wholesome, way to enjoy almonds. The sugar coating makes them unsuitable for grinding into flour but the history of sugared almonds highlights the fact that the benefits of almonds have been well-recognized for many centuries in many different cultures. Now a popular wedding favor around the world, the tradition began with the giving of five Jordan almonds – another name for sugared almonds – to the bride and groom on their wedding day. The five almonds represent fertility, health, happiness, wealth and longevity, and the combination of the nut with the sugar is said to be a representation of the "bitter sweetness" of married life. At a traditional Greek wedding, the sugared almonds are placed in decorative bags and handed out to the guests on silver trays. Each bag contains an odd number of almonds as an odd number cannot be divided, and this is the wish for the new couple as they begin married life. At a traditional Middle Eastern wedding, sugared almonds are freely available and they are thought to be an aphrodisiac!

Making almond flour from almond milk pulp

The left over pulp from making almond milk can also be used to make almond flour. Almond milk is made by soaking the almonds overnight, rinsing them in fresh water, and then blending them in a mix of one part almonds to four parts water until a frothy white liquid is formed. The liquid is then be poured through a strainer to provide almond milk and the solids left behind are the pulp that can be used to make almond flour. By simply spreading the pulp out on a baking tray and placing it in the oven at a low temperature for a few hours, it can be dried out to a consistency that's suitable for grinding up in a blender or coffee grinder. A food dehydrator could also be used in place of an oven for those on a raw food diet, and the dehydrated pulp then ground into flour.

Buying almonds to make your own almond flour

Many grocery stores stock loose almonds, generally without shells, in bulk bins and sell them by the pound. This is very often cheaper than buying packaged almonds but care must be taken to check the quality of the stock each time. Almonds become rancid with age so it's advisable to check how long they have been stored in the bin before purchasing them. Almonds still in their shells will stay fresher for longer than shelled almonds but shaking the shell can tell you a lot about the freshness of the nut inside. If a rattling sound can be heard as you shake it, the almond inside has shrunk in size due to age and is no longer fresh. It's more common to find shelled almonds in grocery stores and it's best to buy from sealed containers rather than open bins whenever possible as exposure to heat and light will also shorten their shelf life. The almonds should smell fresh, be firm to the touch, and have evenly colored skins, so bins that don't smell sweet and nutty or bins containing nuts with mottled skins are best avoided. Almonds are susceptible to mold which appears as a greyish colored layer on the skin and these nuts should not be consumed. A greenish appearance to the skin indicates an immature almond and this too should be avoided as it will have a bitter "unripe" taste. When cut open, the almond should feel firm and have an evenly colored white inner. A spongy texture and yellowish color will be found in rancid almonds and they should not be used.

It's also common to find slivered almonds available in bulk bins and this can be a cost effective and convenient way to purchase them if you intend to use them quickly. Slivered or chopped almonds have a shorter shelf life than whole almonds with their skins still intact but preserving the freshness of all varieties comes down to storing them correctly.

Storing Almonds

The high fat content of almonds means they become rancid quickly if not stored correctly. Shelled almonds can be kept for up to two months when stored in containers with tightly fitting lids and out of direct sunlight in a cool, dry place such as a pantry. Placing them in the refrigerator extends their freshness to around six months and this can be extended further to around one year or even longer by freezing them in airtight containers. Slivered or chopped almonds become rancid faster than whole almonds and are best kept in the refrigerator in airtight containers or vacuum-sealed food storage bags to prevent them from absorbing the odors of other refrigerated foods, and then used within three or four months. As with whole nuts, slivered nuts can also be frozen and will keep for up to one year or more.

Storing Almond Flour

Buying almonds in bulk reduces the cost and makes it possible to always have a supply on hand ready to grind into flour whenever you need it. However, homemade almond flour can also be kept for several months once made, meaning a batch can be ground and then stored away for another day. This is a great way to ensure you always have flour available whenever you need it for baking and cooking and it's much more convenient than having to go out shopping for packaged varieties when your stocks are getting low.

Like whole almonds, freshly ground almond flour can be stored in tightly sealed containers in a dry, cool area of your kitchen for up to two months and placing the containers in the refrigerator extends the freshness for up to six months. It's always a good idea to label and date each batch to ensure it gets used before losing its freshness and a handy tip is to store it in pre-measured amounts in plastic food bags ready for instant use. For example, if your favorite recipes require either one cup or one and a half cups of almond flour, you can place each measured amount into a food bag and mark the measurement on the label before storing it away. Almond flour can also be frozen and kept for a year or so but for best results, the flour should be at room temperature before use. Using it straight from frozen results in a lumpy and unworkable mix so the best approach is to keep a cupboard or pantry supply available for instant use and build up a refrigerator and freezer stock ready for rotation.

Store bought almond flour should be stored in the same way as homemade flour. Transferring it from the packaging into an airtight container such as a glass Mason jar or plastic Tupperware box helps to extend the freshness and also limits the potential for contamination from termites, weevils or mice. It's also important to remember that flour absorbs odors from other foods so keeping an opened package in the refrigerator will extend the freshness but it will not prevent the absorption of odors. Plastic food bags with twist ties are a useful solution for short-term refrigerator storage but containers must be airtight for freezer storage to prevent moisture from coming into contact with the flour.

Substituting Almond Flour in Recipes

Almond flour can be substituted for regular flour in virtually any recipe using flour. However, depending on the recipe, the end result is often denser in texture compared to wheat flour when using almond flour and for this reason many chefs recommend using a mixture of flours to get the best results. For example, if you are not gluten-sensitive, a mix of half wheat flour and half almond flour can bring a delicious moistness and nuttiness to cakes and muffins, or a mix of two-thirds almond flour with one-third wheat flour can really add a nutrient-packed punch to a pizza base.

There are a growing number of recipes specifically designed for almond flour use and therefore there's no guesswork involved in finding the best substitution quantities to use to replace other types of flour. But, in the case of substituting almond flour for any other type of flour, it's generally best to work on a weight-for-weight basis. This means that instead of replacing one cup of regular flour with one cup of almond flour, you need to weigh the contents of one cup of regular flour and then use the same weight of almond flour in its place. For example, if your standard measuring cup holds 4 ounces of wheat flour, you would substitute each cup measurement in the original recipe with 4 ounces of almond flour. This method does require a little more effort to begin with, as well as a set of kitchen scales, but once you have established the weights and how they relate to cup measurements, you can easily go back to using your cup without the need to weigh out the contents each time. Generally, the contents of one cup of almond flour will weigh more than the contents of one cup of wheat flour, meaning a smaller cup measurement of almond flour is needed in place of one cup of wheat flour. From that point forward, it really all comes back to trial-and-error and personal taste. As the saying goes, *"The proof of the pudding is in the eating,"* so if the end result is not what you were hoping for, adjustments can be made for next time.

The type of almond flour you use can also make a significant difference to the end result. In almond flour-specific recipes, the creator of the recipe will very often state the brand of almond flour they used as well as the quantities used, so getting the same end result is dependent on using the same brand and measurements. Of course, even when using regular flour, not every homemade creation is going to turn out exactly like the picture in the recipe book and it's no different when using almond flour!

Little adjustments can make big differences, especially when baking, and every little tweak that may be needed when using regular flour may also be needed when using almond flour. For example, the consistency of a cake mix can vary hugely depending on whether the flour used was sifted or not sifted before being added, or even whether a wooden or metal spoon was used to mix it. The consistency and texture can also be altered by the way the ingredients are measured out. Pouring flour into a measuring cup tends to result in a cupful of packed flour compared to dipping the measuring cup into a container of loose, much less densely packed flour. This in turn will have a direct effect on the actual weights being used which will alter the consistency and texture of the end product.

In conclusion

Almond flour is a delicious and nutritious alternative to regular flour that can be used in cooking and baking to give your food a subtle nutty bite and your body a healthful boost. It is gluten-free, making it ideal for sufferers of Celiac disease or those with gluten-sensitivity; it's low in carbohydrates, making it suitable for those on a carbohydrate restricted diet; it's high in protein, making it a useful addition to a vegetarian diet; it's a Paleo food, making it suitable for those adhering to a Paleo-style diet, and it's a staple ingredient in many raw food recipes, providing a rich source of immune system-boosting antioxidants. And, with its naturally high "healthy" fat content, it is a foodstuff that can help to lower blood cholesterol levels and thereby reduce the risk of developing cardiovascular disease, so all-in-all it's a great tasting "super food" that each and every one of us can enjoy in our daily diet: if you haven't yet tried it, you're missing out!

Soups

1. Almond and Grape Cream with Aromatic Oil

Preparation time	15 minutes
Ready time	15 minutes
Serves	3
Serving quantity/unit	244g / 6.5ounces
Calories	345Cal
Total Fat	36g
Cholesterol	0mg
Sodium	60mg
Total Carbohydrates	9g
Dietary fibers	2g
Sugars	5g
Protein	2g
Vitamin C	4%
Vitamin A	3%
Iron	6%
Calcium	5%

Ingredients

Soup:

- 1 cup of almond flour
- 1 ¾ cup of water
- 3 tbsp. of olive oil
- 1 tbsp. of vinegar
- 1 garlic clove
- 1 cup of grapes of your choice, halved (without seeds)
- 1 pinch of salt

Peppermint oil:

- 1 tbsp. of fresh peppermint, finely chopped
- 1 tbsp. of fresh rosemary, finely chopped
- ¼ cup of olive oil

Method

- Put the ground almond flour in a blender, add the water and garlic. Pulse until smooth and creamy. Add olive oil and vinegar and season with salt.
- To prepare the aromatic oil, combine the herbs with the olive oil.
- Place the grapes in the bottom of soup plates, add the almond cream and a drop of aromatic oil. Serve cold.

Tip – This is a very refreshing and hydrating dish, great for hot summer days.

2. Fresh Apple Cream with Almond Flour and Zucchini

Preparation time	20 minutes
Ready time	20 minutes
Serves	7
Serving quantity/unit	327 g / 11.5 ounces
Calories	220 Cal
Total Fat	15 g
Cholesterol	0 mg
Sodium	370 mg
Total Carbohydrates	18g
Dietary fibers	4g
Sugars	9g
Protein	7g
Vitamin C	36%
Vitamin A	13%
Iron	9%
Calcium	7%

Ingredients

- ¼ cup of olive oil
- 2 garlic cloves, minced
- 2 leeks, white part only sliced
- 2 large zucchinis, cubed
- 2 Granny Smith apples, cored, peeled and cubed
- 3 cups of vegetable stock

- 3 tbsps. of almond flour
- 3 tbsps. of sliced almonds
- 1 pinch of salt, black pepper and nutmeg

Method

- Heat the olive oil and garlic in a pan, add the leeks and cook covered for 4 minutes. Add the zucchinis. Cook for further 3 minutes.
- Add the apples and the vegetable stock, cover and let simmer over low heat until the vegetables are tender.
- Add the almond flour, if necessary, adjust the consistency adding more water (to make it less thick) or cooking for a longer period (to thicken). Add a pinch of salt, pepper and nutmeg.
- Remove from heat, let cool and transfer to a blender. Pulse until smooth and creamy.
- Let cool completely (keep it in the fridge until serving).
- Right before serving, toast the sliced almonds in a nonstick skillet over medium heat (around 3 minutes) and distribute them for the soup bowls.

Tip – This cream is an excellent source of vitamin C and a good source of vitamin A.

3. Almond and Saffron Soup

Preparation time	20 minutes
Ready time	20 minutes
Serves	4
Serving quantity/unit	250 g / 9 ounces
Calories	227 Cal
Total Fat	17g
Cholesterol	0 mg
Sodium	646mg
Total Carbohydrates	17g
Dietary fibers	5g
Sugars	2g
Protein	8g
Vitamin C	8%
Vitamin A	5%
Iron	7%
Calcium	4%

Ingredients

- 1 cup of almond flour
- 3 to 4 slices of paleo bread, cubed
- 4 garlic cloves, minced

- 3 tbsps. of fresh parsley
- 3 cups of vegetable stock
- 3 tbsps. of olive oil
- 1 tsp. ground cumin
- 1 tsp. of saffron threads
- Salt and pepper

Method

- Heat the oil in a large skillet, add the bread and cook until golden, stirring occasionally.
- Remove the bread and place it on paper towels to drain the excess fat.
- Put the garlic and parsley in the skillet and sauté for 2 or 3 minutes (add a little more oil if necessary).
- Transfer to a food processor, add almond flour and half of the bread and pulse until a paste forms.
- Pour the pulp obtained into a pan, add the cumin and saffron and stir in the vegetable stock gradually, stirring constantly.
- Bring to a boil. Reduce the heat, cover the pan and simmer for about 20 minutes stirring occasionally. If necessary, add more vegetable broth or water.
- Add a pinch of salt and pepper and serve garnished with bread cubes and a sprinkle of parsley.

Tip – Did you know that parsley is a great source of iron, manganese and magnesium? It is also an excellent source of vitamins, just 2 tbsps. can provide up to 15% of the daily recommendations of vitamin A and up to 20% of the daily recommendations of vitamin C.

4. Warm Broccoli and Almond Soup

Preparation time	30 minutes
Ready time	30 minutes
Serves	6
Serving quantity/unit	390 G / 14 ounces
Calories	114 Cal
Total Fat	5G
Cholesterol	0mg
Sodium	826mg
Total Carbohydrates	10G
Dietary fibers	4G
Sugars	4G
Protein	9G
Vitamin C	177%
Vitamin A	8%
Iron	9%
Calcium	3%

Ingredients

- 1/2 cup of almond flour
- 1 onion, finely chopped
- 1 garlic clove, minced
- 1 tbsp. of olive oil
- 1 head of broccoli
- ½ head of cauliflower
- 6 cups of vegetable stock
- Salt, pepper and nutmeg to taste

Method

- Peel the broccoli stems. Cut stems and florets into small pieces. Repeat the process for the cauliflower. Set aside.
- Toast the almond flour in a non-stick skillet over low heat until it becomes fragrant and golden. Remove from heat, set aside.
- Heat the oil in a large pot over medium heat. Add the onion and garlic and cook for 3-4 minutes. Add the broccoli and cauliflower pieces and cook for 7-10 minutes
- Add the vegetable stock and bring to a boil. Lower the heat and let simmer for 10-15 minutes or until the vegetables are tender.
- Add the almond flour, season and puree the soup.

Tip – Toast a spoonful of chopped almonds and add them to your soup with a squeeze of lemon juice and a tsp. of fresh basil to get new flavor and texture dimensions.

Vegetarian

5. Almond Flour Bread

Preparation time	50 minutes
Ready time	1 hour 30 minutes
Serves	6
Serving quantity/unit	80G / 3 ounces
Calories	141Cal
Total Fat	13G
Cholesterol	55mg
Sodium	136mg
Total Carbohydrates	3G
Dietary fibers	2G
Sugars	1G
Protein	5G
Vitamin C	0%
Vitamin A	1%
Iron	5%
Calcium	3%

Ingredients

- 2 ½ cups of almond flour
- ¼ cup of almond milk
- 2 eggs, yolks and whites separated
- 1 ½ tbsps. of olive oil
- ½ tsp. of sodium bicarbonate
- ¼ teaspoon of salt

Method

- Preheat the oven to 350°F.
- Grease an oven-safe pan with oil and line it with parchment paper.
- Combine all the remaining ingredients (except egg whites) in a mixing bowl.

- Beat the egg whites until stiff and carefully fold them in the yolk mixture.
- Refrigerate for 30-40 minutes.
- Pour the batter into the prepared pan and bake for 30 minutes or until a toothpick comes out clean.

Tip – There are several ingredients you can use to enrich the nutritional content of this bread. Nutritional yeast is a great source of iron and protein, sesame seeds are good sources of calcium and sunflower seeds are packed with micronutrients such as magnesium, selenium, phosphorus, and manganese.

6. Savory Crackers

Preparation time	15 minutes
Ready time	30 minutes
Serves	6
Serving quantity/unit	30g / 1 ounce
Calories	69Cal
Total Fat	7g
Cholesterol	0mg
Sodium	30mg
Total Carbohydrates	2g
Dietary fibers	1g
Sugars	0g
Protein	1g
Vitamin C	2%
Vitamin A	1%
Iron	2%
Calcium	2%

Ingredients

- 1 cup of almond flour
- 2 tbsps. of cold water
- 2 tsps. of coconut oil
- 1 pinch of salt
- 1 tbsp. of dried tomatoes
- ¼ tsp. of sweet paprika
- 1 tsp. of black pepper
- 1 tsp. of oregano

Method

- Preheat the oven to 350ºF.

- Line a baking tray with parchment paper.
- Combine all the ingredients in a food processor and pulse until smooth.
- Scoop small portions of dough onto baking tray and bake for 15 minutes.

Tip – For a different flavor, try making these crackers with a couple tablespoons of pesto sauce.

7. Vegetarian Loaf

Preparation time	40minutes
Ready time	1hour 30 minutes
Serves	4
Serving quantity/unit	304G / 11 ounces
Calories	432Cal
Total Fat	34g
Cholesterol	82mg
Sodium	291mg
Total Carbohydrates	23g
Dietary fibers	7g
Sugars	9g
Protein	17g
Vitamin C	18%
Vitamin A	4%
Iron	20%
Calcium	17%

Ingredients

Loaf

- 2 tablespoons of coconut oil
- 1 onion, chopped
- 3 stalks of celery
- 1 cup of vegetable stock
- 1 cup of almond flour
- 2 slices of paleo bread
- 1 tablespoon of flaxseed meal softened in 3 tbsps. of warm water
- 1 grated apple
- 2 eggs
- Juice of ½ a lemon
- Salt and pepper to taste

Filling

- 1 tablespoon of coconut oil
- 1 onion, chopped
- 1 cup of diced mushrooms
- ½ cup of walnuts, chopped
- ¼ cup of sesame seeds
- 3 garlic cloves, minced

Method

- Place the bread in a food processor and blend into breadcrumbs. Set aside.
- Heat the oil in a skillet and sauté the onion for 5 minutes or until softened.
- Add the celery and cook for further 5 minutes.
- Sprinkle with flaxseed meal and cook adding small portions of vegetable stock at a time until you've used all the broth.
- Add the lemon juice. Pour this mixture over the almonds, and mix to combine.
- Season with salt and pepper.
- To make the filling, heat the oil and sauté the onion for 3 minutes or until soft, add the mushrooms and cook for another 10 minutes
- Grease a rectangular oven-safe dish and line it with baking paper. Pour half of the almond mixture onto the baking dish and spread it evenly.
- Add the mushroom sauté and the other filling ingredients.
- Pour the remaining mixture on top.
- Bake in a preheated oven at 190 °C for about 50 minutes or until golden.

Tip – It's possible to make endless variations of this dish just by substituting the ingredients.

8. "Breaded" Tomatoes

Preparation time	15 minutes
Ready time	30 minutes
Serves	2
Serving quantity/unit	190g / 7ounces
Calories	325Cal
Total Fat	29g
Cholesterol	82mg
Sodium	67mg
Total Carbohydrates	12g
Dietary fibers	6g
Sugars	5g
Protein	10g
Vitamin C	28%
Vitamin A	27%
Iron	16%
Calcium	13%

Ingredients

- 2 fresh tomatoes, sliced
- 1 egg
- 1 tsp. mustard
- 1 tbsp. of dried oregano
- 1 tbsp. of fresh basil, finely chopped
- ½ cup of almond flour
- 2 tbsps. of olive oil
- salt and pepper

Method

- Slice the tomatoes.
- Whisk together egg and mustard.
- Combine the almond flour and herbs, in a mixing bowl. Season with salt and pepper.
- Dip the tomato slices in the egg.
- Place each tomato slice in the almond flour bowl and toss to coat.
- Heat the olive oil in a large skillet over medium heat, add the tomato slices and cook until golden on both sides.

Tip – Did you know that tomato is not a vegetable? It's a fruit, and a very nutritious one, it's packed with essential minerals, vitamins and important anti-oxidants.

9. Paleo Buns

Preparation time	45minutes
Ready time	1hour
Serves	7
Serving quantity/unit	66 g / 2 ounces
Calories	157Cal
Total Fat	15g
Cholesterol	94mg
Sodium	387mg
Total Carbohydrates	3g
Dietary fibers	1g
Sugars	1g
Protein	5g
Vitamin C	1%
Vitamin A	3%
Iron	6%
Calcium	3%

Ingredients

- 1 cup of almond flour
- 1 tsp. of baking soda
- 1 tbsp. of flax seed softened in 3 tbsps. of warm water
- 1 tbsp. of sunflower seeds
- 1 tsp. of ground cumin
- 1/2 teaspoon of salt
- ½ cup of almond milk
- 4 eggs, whisked
- 3 tablespoons of coconut oil, melted

Method

- Combine all the dry ingredients in a large bowl.
- Add the eggs and mix. Add the milk and coconut oil and blend until the mixture is homogenous. Let sit for 30 minutes.
- Pre-heat oven to 200°C.
- Divide the mixture into 7 portions and shape them into balls
- Bake in for 15 minutes or until a toothpick comes out clean.

Tip – If you're craving something sweeter, try substituting almond milk for coconut milk, and ground cumin for vanilla essence.

10. Vegetarian Lasagna

Preparation time	45minutes
Ready time	1hour 30minutes
Serves	8
Serving quantity/unit	350g/ 12 ounces
Calories	432Cal
Total Fat	35g
Cholesterol	0mg
Sodium	629mg
Total Carbohydrates	26g
Dietary fibers	11g
Sugars	9g
Protein	11g
Vitamin C	26%
Vitamin A	47%
Iron	26%
Calcium	13%

Ingredients

Lasagna

- 2 eggplants
- 3 leeks (white part only) finely sliced
- 1 large carrot, grated
- 1 onion, minced
- 2 cups of almonds, chopped
- 2 tomatoes, peeled and chopped
- 3 tbsps. of olive oil
- Salt, pepper and dried oregano

Lasagna sauce

- 1 cup almond milk
- 4 tbsps. of almond flour
- 2 garlic cloves, minced
- ½ cup of mushrooms
- Salt, pepper and nutmeg to taste.
- 2 tbsps. of olive oil

Method

- Cut the eggplants into very thin slices using a mandolin. Sprinkle with salt and let rest for 15-20 minutes to remove the juices.
- Heat 2 tablespoons of olive oil in a large skillet over medium-high heat and grill the eggplant slices.
- Prepare the filling: heat 1 tbsp. of olive oil in a large skillet over medium heat. Sauté de onion for 2-3 minutes, add the tomatoes, carrot and leeks.
- Season with salt, pepper and oregano. Cook for 10-15 minutes.
- Remove from heat. Stir in the almonds. Set aside
- To prepare the sauce, heat the olive oil in a non-stick skillet, over medium heat, add the chopped mushrooms, garlic, salt and pepper and sauté for 7-10 minutes.
- Transfer to a food processor and pulse until smooth.
- Pour in the milk and almond flour, pulse until homogeneous.
- Season with nutmeg and, if necessary, more salt and pepper.
- Pre-heat the oven to 350F.
- Assemble the lasagna: Cover the bottom of a medium-size, oven-safe dish with grilled eggplant slices, add some vegetable filling and top it with the lasagna sauce. Repeat this process until you've used all the filling. Cover the last filling layer with eggplant slices and sauce.
- Bake for 20-30 minutes.

Tip- this is a great source of fiber, vitamin A, manganese and vitamin B6.

11. Zucchini Noodles with Almond and Basil Pesto Sauce

Preparation time	30minutes
Ready time	30 minutes
Serves	4
Serving quantity/unit	240g / 8 ounces
Calories	350Cal
Total Fat	34g
Cholesterol	6mg
Sodium	1279mg
Total Carbohydrates	9g
Dietary fibers	3g
Sugars	3g
Protein	7g
Vitamin C	45%
Vitamin A	6%
Iron	7%
Calcium	13%

Ingredients

Noodles

- 3 zucchinis
- 2 tsps. of salt

Pesto

- 3 cups of fresh basil
- 1 cup of almond flour
- 1 ¼ cup olive oil
- Juice of half a lemon
- 4 garlic cloves
- ½ cup parmesan cheese (optional)
- Salt and pepper to taste

Method

- Cut the zucchini into very thin slices using a mandolin or vegetable peeler and then julienne the slices.
- Transfer to a colander, add salt, and let sit for 20 to 30 minutes to dry out the zucchini.
- Squeeze out the excess water, and pat dry the noodles.
- To prepare the pesto, toast the almond flour in the oven, at 300F for 5 to 10 minutes (until golden).
- Remove from the oven and let cool.
- Transfer to a food processor, add the basil, lemon juice and garlic (and the parmesan cheese if you choose to use it) and pulse until homogeneous.
- Pour in ¼ of olive oil, pulse to combine. Repeat until you've used all the oil.
- Season with salt and pepper.
- Serve the noodles with a spoonful of pesto on top.

Tip – For a new flavor, sauté the noodles for 5 minutes, to get an extra crunch, sprinkle your dish with your favorite toasted nuts and/or seeds.

Fish

12. Paleo Fish Cakes

Preparation time	30 minutes
Ready time	1 hour
Serves	4
Serving quantity/unit	300G / 10.5ounces
Calories	494Cal
Total Fat	36g
Cholesterol	153mg
Sodium	713mg
Total Carbohydrates	14g
Dietary fibers	5g
Sugars	5g
Protein	32g
Vitamin C	85%
Vitamin A	33%
Iron	26%
Calcium	8%

Ingredients

- 1 pound of salmon, or a mixture of salmon and another fish of your choice
- 1 cup of cauliflower florets
- ½ cup of red bell pepper, chopped
- 5 sprigs of chopped cilantro
- 5 sprigs of chopped parsley
- 1 leek (white part only), sliced
- ½ cup of almond flour
- ½ cup of dried, unsweetened coconut
- 2 eggs
- 1 cup of coconut milk
- Zest of 1 lemon
- Juice of ½ a lemon

- 1 garlic clove
- 1 tbsp. of freshly grated ginger
- Salt and pepper to taste

Method

- Preheat oven to 300F.
- Put the cauliflower in a pot, cover with water, season with salt and bring to a boil over medium heat. Lower the heat and let simmer until tender.
- Remove from heat, let cool and transfer the cauliflower to a blender.
- Cut the fish into small pieces, discard the skin and bones, and put it in the blender with the cauliflower florets.
- Pour in the coconut milk and pulse until homogeneous.
- Add the remaining ingredients, and, once again, pulse until homogenous.
- Scoop small portions of the mixture into non-stick muffin cups.
- Bake for 20 to 30 minutes or until completely cooked

Tip – This dish is a great source of selenium, several B vitamins. It is packed with vitamins A and C, providing 1/3 of the recommended daily amount of vitamin A and satisfying ¾ of the daily needs of vitamin C.

13. Perch Fillet with Coconut Milk Sauce

Preparation time	1 hour 10minutes
Ready time	1hour 30 minutes
Serves	4
Serving quantity/unit	177g / 6ounces
Calories	226Cal
Total Fat	13g
Cholesterol	45mg
Sodium	680mg
Total Carbohydrates	4g
Dietary fibers	2g
Sugars	1g
Protein	24g
Vitamin C	6%
Vitamin A	0%
Iron	14%
Calcium	12%

Ingredients

- 4 perch fillets
- ½ cup of coconut milk
- Juice of ½ lemon
- 1 tablespoon of almond flour
- 1 tsp. of dried coriander
- ½ tsp. of dried ginger
- 2 teaspoons of turmeric
- A pinch of salt and pepper

Method

- Place the fish in a mixing bowl, add the coconut milk, salt, pepper, coriander, and ginger.
- Cover with cling film and refrigerate for 1 hour.
- Heat a non-stick skillet over medium-heat, and cook the fish fillets for 3-5 minutes on each side (reserve the marinate liquid).
- Put the turmeric and almond flour in a saucepan, pour in the fish marinate liquid stirring to combine. Bring to a simmer over low heat, and cook for 3-5 minutes.
- Pour over the perch fillets and serve.

Tip – to get a thicker sauce, add a little more almond flour, if you prefer it less dense, add an extra spoonful of coconut milk. Serve with cauliflower rice and a fresh green salad.

14. Salmon with Black Olive and Almond Crust

Preparation time	40 minutes
Ready time	1 hour
Serves	4
Serving quantity/unit	200g / 7 ounces
Calories	465Cal
Total Fat	32g
Cholesterol	112mg
Sodium	963mg
Total Carbohydrates	3g
Dietary fibers	0g
Sugars	0g
Protein	40g
Vitamin C	18%
Vitamin A	2%
Iron	4%
Calcium	4%

Ingredients

- 4 salmon steaks
- 2 tbsps. of black olive paste
- ¼ cup almond flour
- Juice of ½ a lemon
- 3 cloves of garlic, minced
- 2 tbsps. of olive oil
- Salt
- Pepper

Method

- Combine the olive oil, half of the lemon juice, salt and pepper in a mixing bowl. Marinate the salmon in the mixture for 20-30 minutes.
- Pre-heat oven to 350F.
- Put the almond flour, black olive paste, garlic and the remaining lemon juice in a blender and pulse until homogeneous.
- Transfer the salmon fillets to an oven-safe dish. Spread one spoon of the olive mixture over each salmon steak and bake for 15-20 minutes.

Tip – Sautéed asparagus and a couscous salad are a perfect match for this salmon.

15. Oven Baked Cod

Preparation time	40 minutes
Ready time	1hour
Serves	4
Serving quantity/unit	273g / 10ounces
Calories	329Cal
Total Fat	23G
Cholesterol	42mg
Sodium	mg
Total Carbohydrates	15g
Dietary fibers	5g
Sugars	5g
Protein	23g
Vitamin C	52%
Vitamin A	0%
Iron	5%
Calcium	7%

Ingredients

- 3 cod fillets
- 6 garlic cloves, minced
- 3 onions, finely sliced
- ¼ cup + 1 tbsp. of olive oil
- 2 slices of Paleo bread of your choice
- ½ cup of almond flour
- 2 cups of sliced cauliflower florets (boiled and drained)
- Salt and pepper to taste

Method

- Put the cod in a large pan, cover with water and bring to a boil over medium heat.
- Simmer for 10-15 minutes or until cooked.
- Pre-heat oven to 350F.
- Remove from heat, drain and let cool. Discard the skin and bones.
- Using your hands, flake the cod steaks into bite size pieces.
- Heat ¼ cup of oil in a pot over medium heat. Add the onions and garlic and sauteé for 5-7 minutes or until the onion is golden.
- Stir in the cod flakes. Season with salt and pepper.
- Cover the bottom of an oven safe dish with the cauliflower. Spread the onion and cauliflower mix on top. Set aside.
- Crumble the bread in a food processor.
- Heat 1 tbsp. of oil in a non-stick skillet over low heat. Add the almond flour and toast it for 2 minutes. Stir in the bread crumbs. Remove from heat. Let cool and sprinkle it over the cod and onion mixture.
- Bake for 20 minutes or until golden.

Tip – Cod usually goes very well with creamy sauces. For a whole new flavor, prepare this dish without the onions, make a sauce simmering 1 cup of almond milk, 3 tbsps. of almond flour, salt, pepper and nutmeg (over low heat for 5-10 minutes or until it thickens) and pour it over the cod in the baking dish before putting it in the oven.

16. Mediterranean Swordfish Steaks

Preparation time	40 minutes
Ready time	1hour
Serves	4
Serving quantity/unit	360g / 13 ounces
Calories	417 Cal
Total Fat	27g
Cholesterol	136mg
Sodium	801mg
Total Carbohydrates	9g
Dietary fibers	4g
Sugars	3g
Protein	37g
Vitamin C	26%
Vitamin A	17%
Iron	15%
Calcium	8%

Ingredients

- 4 swordfish steaks
- 50 g of almond flour
- 1 tablespoon of parsley
- 2 tbsps. of olive oil
- 2 tomatoes, peeled and cubed
- 1 cup of fish stock
- 2 eggs, whisked
- juice of 1 lemon
- 3 garlic cloves
- 3 tbsps. of almond flour
- salt

Method

- Pre-heat oven to 350F.
- Wash and dry the steaks.
- Transfer to a mixing bowl, season with salt and lemon juice and set aside.
- Combine the garlic, almond flour, parsley and one tbsp. of oil in a food processor and pulse until homogeneous.
- Heat the remaining oil in a large skillet over medium heat, add the tomatoes, cook for 5 minutes.

- Stir in the fish stock and the garlic and almond flour mixture. Let simmer for 5-7 minutes.
- Remove from heat, let cool and add the eggs, stir to combine.
- Place the fish in an oven-safe dish, pour over the sauce and bake for 30-40 minutes or until the fish is fully cooked.

Tip – Serve with a fresh tomato, black olive and basil salad, drizzled with extra-virgin olive oil and seasoned with salt and black pepper.

You can replace swordfish for other types of firm white fish.

Meat

17. Spiced Muffins

Preparation time	30minutes
Ready time	1hour
Serves	12
Serving quantity/unit	102g / 4 ounces
Calories	118Cal
Total Fat	9G
Cholesterol	48mg
Sodium	416mg
Total Carbohydrates	5g
Dietary fibers	2g
Sugars	2g
Protein	5g
Vitamin C	35%
Vitamin A	14%
Iron	6%
Calcium	4%

Ingredients

Crust

- 1 cup of almond flour
- 2 eggs
- 3 tbsps. of olive oil
- 2 tbsps. of chia seeds flour
- 1 zucchini

Filling

- 1 pound of ground beef
- 1 egg

- 3 tomatoes, peeled
- 1 green bell pepper, chopped
- 1 onion, finely chopped
- 2 garlic cloves, minced
- 1 tablespoon of olive oil
- 1 tablespoon of chopped parsley
- 1 tablespoon of chopped basil
- Salt and pepper to taste

Method

- Grate the zucchini, place it in a colander and press to remove as more liquid as possible.
- Transfer to a mixing bowl and add the remaining ingredients for the crust
- Let sit for 30 minutes. If needed, add more almond flour to adjust consistency.
- Grease 12 muffin cups with olive oil and line them with the crust mixture.
- Put the muffin cups in a pre-heated oven at 200ºC for 10 minutes.
- To prepare the filling, sauté de onions and garlic in the olive oil for 3 minutes over medium heat. Add the tomatoes, bell pepper and meat and sauté until the meat is fully cooked.
- Season with salt and pepper.
- Remove from heat, let cool. Incorporate the egg and fresh herbs in the mixture.
- Fill the previously prepared muffin cups with the meat mixture and put them bake in the oven, at 180 ºC, for 15 minutes or until golden.

Tip – These muffins are great sources of vitamins A and C.

18. Beef Medallion with an Herb Crust

Preparation time	15 minutes
Ready time	30 minutes
Serves	4
Serving quantity/unit	153g / 5 ounces
Calories	433Cal
Total Fat	33g
Cholesterol	78mg
Sodium	642mg
Total Carbohydrates	11g
Dietary fibers	7g
Sugars	0g
Protein	27g
Vitamin C	17%
Vitamin A	15%
Iron	36%
Calcium	23%

Ingredients

- 4 steaks of beef tenderloin
- 2 tablespoons of olive oil
- salt

Crust:

- 1 cup of almond flour
- ¼ cup of olive oil
- 1 cup of basil leaves
- 1 cup of fresh rosemary
- salt and pepper to taste

Method

- Pre-heat oven to 350F.
- Season the medallions with salt and pepper.
- Put all the crust ingredients in a food processor and pulse until homogeneous.
- Heat the olive oil in a skillet over high heat and sear the medallions (2 at a time) over until browned on one side. Turn and brown the other side.
- Divide the crust mixture into 4 portions and place one portion over each medallion (pressing well).
- Transfer to a baking sheet and bake for 5 minutes or until the crust is golden brown.

Tip –Use a mandolin to cut thin slices of zucchini and fry them in olive oil or another oil of your choice. Serve the medallions with the zucchini chips and a fresh salad

19. Ham and Spinach Stuffed Chicken Breasts

Preparation time	20Minutes
Ready time	50 minutes
Serves	2
Serving quantity/unit	270g / 10ounces
Calories	543Cal
Total Fat	33G
Cholesterol	237mg
Sodium	1121mg
Total Carbohydrates	6g
Dietary fibers	2g
Sugars	1g
Protein	57g
Vitamin C	21%
Vitamin A	81%
Iron	26%
Calcium	11%

Ingredients

- 2 chicken breasts
- 2 slices of good quality prosciutto
- 8 spinach leaves
- 1 egg, whisked
- 1/4 cup of almond flour
- 2 tbsps. of olive oil
- 2 tsps. of dried oregano
- 2 tsps. of garlic powder
- Salt and pepper
- kitchen string

Method

- Pre-heat oven to 400F.
- Make an incision in the edge of each chicken breast to create a pocket (be careful not to cut through the other side).
- Cut the prosciutto into smaller pieces that will fit inside the "pocket".
- Stuff each breast with the prosciutto and spinach leaves. Use the kitchen string to wrap them.
- In a mixing bowl, combine the almond flour, oregano, garlic powder and a pinch of salt and pepper.
- Oil the center of a baking sheet.

- Dip the chicken breasts into the whisked egg, coating all sides, then into the almond mixture, coating all sides.
- Lay them on the baking sheet.
- Drizzle the remaining olive oil over the top of the chicken breasts and bake for 30 minutes or until the crust is golden and the chicken fully cooked.
- Remove from the oven and let cool. Cut the string and remove it before serving.

Tip – If you eat dairy, add a slice of your favorite cheese to the filling to make this dish extra-tasty. Alternatively, you can use a combination of different hams to get new layers of flavor and add some drops of almond milk to the stuffing for additional creaminess.

20. Veal Scallops with Creamy Almond Sauce

Preparation time	15 minutes
Ready time	30 minutes
Serves	4
Serving quantity/unit	220G / 8 ounces
Calories	314Cal
Total Fat	23g
Cholesterol	88mg
Sodium	944mg
Total Carbohydrates	3g
Dietary fibers	1g
Sugars	1g
Protein	26g
Vitamin C	1%
Vitamin A	0%
Iron	8%
Calcium	3%

Ingredients

- 4 3oz. veal sirloin steaks
- 3 tbsps. of olive oil
- ¾ cup of almond flour
- ¼ tsp. of ground cinnamon
- 1 ½ cup of chicken broth
- ¼ cup of almond milk
- ½ tsp. of nutmeg
- Salt and white pepper to taste

Method

- Heat the oil in a large skillet, add the scallops, season with salt and cook for 3-5 minutes on each side or until golden-brown.
- Transfer the scallops to a plate and heat the same skillet (with the remaining juices) over medium heat. Add the almond flour and cook until golden.
- Gradually add the milk and broth to the mixture, stirring constantly until the sauce thickens. Season with nutmeg, salt and pepper.
- Add the scallops, bring to a simmer and cook for 3-5 minutes.

Tip – Add some fresh, chopped mushrooms to the sauce for a whole different flavor.

21. Low-carb Turkey Meatballs

Preparation time	30minutes
Ready time	50 minutes
Serves	4
Serving quantity/unit	250G / 9 ounces
Calories	497Cal
Total Fat	35g
Cholesterol	157mg
Sodium	164mg
Total Carbohydrates	10g
Dietary fibers	3g
Sugars	4g
Protein	35g
Vitamin C	16%
Vitamin A	19%
Iron	22%
Calcium	7%

Ingredients

Meatballs

- 1 pound of ground turkey
- ½ cup of almond flour
- 3 garlic cloves, minced
- 1 egg
- 1 tbsp. of oregano
- 1 tbsp. of basil
- 2 tsps. of your favorite spice mix
- 4 tbsps. of olive oil

Sauce

- 1 cup of pure tomato puree
- 1 onion, finely chopped
- 1 garlic clove, minced
- 1 bay leaf
- Salt to taste
- 1 tbsp. of olive oil

Method

- In a mixing bowl, combine the ground turkey, garlic, egg, almond flour, fresh herbs and spices (add salt if needed).
- Divide the mixture into small portions and form the meatballs.
- Heat the oil in a large, non-stick skillet and sauté the meatballs over medium heat for 7-10minutes turning them to avoid burning.
- Remove from heat, let cool.
- To prepare the sauce, heat the olive oil in a skillet over medium heat. Add the onion and garlic and sauté until translucent.
- Add the bay leaf, salt and tomato pulp. Bring to a gentle boil, lower the heat and let simmer for 2-5 minutes. Add the meatballs and cook for further 5-10minutes. If necessary, add a little water or more tomato pulp to adjust sauce consistency.

Tip – To get a dish with an entirely different flavor, add the juice of half a lemon to the ground turkey mix and use fresh parsley and coriander instead of the herbs in the recipe.

22. Bacon Quiche

Preparation time	1 hour
Ready time	1hour 30 minutes
Serves	4
Serving quantity/unit	170g / 6 ounces
Calories	344Cal
Total Fat	30G
Cholesterol	139mg
Sodium	586mg
Total Carbohydrates	6g
Dietary fibers	4g
Sugars	2g
Protein	14g
Vitamin C	50%
Vitamin A	19%
Iron	13%
Calcium	8%

Ingredients

Crust:
- **1 egg**
- **2 Cups of almond flour**
- **2 Tablespoon of flaxseed**
- **2 Tablespoons of olive oil**
- **3 tbsps. of warm water**
- **Salt to taste**

Filling:

- ½ cup of bacon, chopped
- 1 cup of green bell pepper, chopped
- ½ cup of black olives
- 2 Tablespoons almond milk
- ½ tbsp. of olive oil
- 2 eggs, whisked
- salt and pepper

Method

- Grind flax seeds in a food processor until a fine powder forms. Transfer to a small mixing bowl. Pour in the water and let sit for 20minutes.
- Meanwhile, start preparing the filling by heating the oil in a non-stick skillet over medium heat. Add the bacon and green pepper and cook for 5 minutes. Stir in the olives, cook for further 5 minutes. Remove from heat and let cool.
- Continue preparing the crust by combining all the remaining crust ingredients in a large mixing bowl. Add the flax seed mixture and, if necessary, add more almond flour to adjust consistency.
- Wrap in plastic film and refrigerate for at least fifteen minutes.
- Pre-heat oven to 350F.
- Back to the filling, whisk together eggs and milk. Season with salt and pepper. Stir in the bacon mixture.
- Grease a pie pan with olive oil and line it with non-stick baking paper.
- Using the palm of your hand, press the dough into the pie pan and poke the crust with a fork.
- Pour in the filling and bake for 20-30 minutes or until golden.

Tip – There are innumerous variations of this dish. It's usually a great way to use leftovers such as the roasted meat and vegetables from Sunday night's dinner and create a meal that tastes anything but leftovers.

23. Home-made Hamburger

Preparation time	15 minutes
Ready time	30minutes
Serves	6
Serving quantity/unit	195g / 7 ounces
Calories	308Cal
Total Fat	15G
Cholesterol	129mg
Sodium	477mg
Total Carbohydrates	5g
Dietary fibers	2g
Sugars	3g
Protein	37g
Vitamin C	70%
Vitamin A	21%
Iron	122%
Calcium	3%

Ingredients

- 1 ½ pounds of lean ground beef
- ½ cup of almond flour
- 1 large onion, minced
- 1 cup of green bell pepper, chopped
- 1 cup of red bell pepper, chopped
- 1 egg
- 1 tbsp. of parsley
- 2 tbsps. of flaxseed
- 1 tsp. of black pepper
- 1 tsp. of garlic powder
- 1 tsp. of salt
- 2 tbsps. of olive oil

Method

- Combine all the ingredients (except olive oil) in a large bowl.
- Divide the dough into small balls and press them using the palm of your hands to create a hamburger shape.
- Heat the oil in a large skillet over medium heat. Add the hamburgers and cook for 5-7 minutes on each side, or until fully cooked.

Tip – These hamburgers are excellent sources of minerals such as iron, phosphorus, selenium and zinc.

Desserts, Cakes, Muffins, and Other Sweet Treats

24. Orange Cake

Preparation time	30minutes
Ready time	1hour
Serves	6
Serving quantity/unit	122G / 4 ounces
Calories	247Cal
Total Fat	9g
Cholesterol	109mg
Sodium	42mg
Total Carbohydrates	40g
Dietary fibers	1g
Sugars	37g
Protein	5g
Vitamin C	46%
Vitamin A	5%
Iron	4%
Calcium	3%

Ingredients

Cake

- 4 eggs, yolks and whites separated
- ½ cup of raw sugar
- ½ cup of almond flour
- zest of 1 orange
- 2 tbsps. of coconut oil, melted

Orange syrup

- 1 cup of orange juice
- ½ cup of raw sugar

Method

- Preheat the oven to 350°F.
- Grease a cake pan with a tbsp. of coconut oil and line it with non-stick baking paper.
- Combine the yolks, the remaining oil, orange zest and sugar in a large bowl. Stir in almond flour.
- Beat the egg whites until stiff and carefully fold them in the cake batter.
- Pour the batter into the cake pan and bake for 30 minutes or until a toothpick comes out clean.
- Meanwhile, prepare the syrup by combining the orange juice and raw sugar in a saucepan and bringing it to a simmer over low heat. Let cook for 5 minutes. Remove from heat and let cool.
- After removing the cake from the oven, poke it all over with a fork and pour the prepared syrup over hot cake.
- Let cool and turn onto a serving plate

Tip – For a fresh summer cake, add two tablespoons of finely chopped fresh basil to the batter.

25. Surprise Muffins

Preparation time	30minutes
Ready time	50 minutes
Serves	10 muffins
Serving quantity/unit	1 muffin/ 110g / 4 ounces
Calories	311Cal
Total Fat	24g
Cholesterol	65mg
Sodium	159mg
Total Carbohydrates	24g
Dietary fibers	1g
Sugars	22g
Protein	4g
Vitamin C	2%
Vitamin A	2%
Iron	7%
Calcium	3%

Ingredients

- 1 ½ cups of coconut milk
- ½ cup of coconut oil, melted
- 4 eggs, yolks and whites separated
- ¾ cup of raw honey
- 2 cups of almond flour

- 1 tsp. of baking soda

Method

- Preheat the oven to 350F.
- Combine the yolks, oil, and honey in a large bowl and add the coconut milk.
- Mix flour with baking soda and add to the egg mixture.
- Beat the egg whites until stiff and carefully fold them in the cake batter.
- Pour the batter into 10 muffin paper liners, and bake for 15-20 minutes or until muffins are light golden brown.

Tip – The interior of these muffins will be soft and moist, so it is important not to leave them in the oven for too long. Serve them with toasted walnuts and some pieces of dried coconut on top for additional texture.

26. Chocolate Brownies

Preparation time	30minutes
Ready time	1hour
Serves	9
Serving quantity/unit	100g / 3.5 ounces
Calories	305Cal
Total Fat	22g
Cholesterol	73mg
Sodium	172mg
Total Carbohydrates	27g
Dietary fibers	3g
Sugars	23g
Protein	6g
Vitamin C	0%
Vitamin A	2%
Iron	8%
Calcium	4%

Ingredients

- 1 cup of raw sugar
- 1/2 cup of unsweetened cocoa powder
- ½ cup of coconut oil + 1 tbsp., melted
- 4 eggs, yolks and whites separated
- 3.5 oz. of almond flour
- 1 tsp. of baking soda

Method

- Preheat the oven to 350°F.
- Grease a cake pan with 1 tbsp. of oil and line it with non-stick baking paper.
- Combine the remaining oil, sugar and yolks in a mixing bowl.
- Blend in the almond flour, cocoa and sodium bicarbonate.
- Beat the egg whites until stiff and carefully fold them in the cake batter.
- Pour the batter into the cake pan and bake for 30-35 minutes.

Tip – Serve while still warm with slices of fresh strawberries.

27. Apple Crunch

Preparation time	30 minutes
Ready time	1 hour
Serves	10
Serving quantity/unit	155g / 5 ounces
Calories	245Cal
Total Fat	13g
Cholesterol	0mg
Sodium	3mg
Total Carbohydrates	33g
Dietary fibers	4g
Sugars	28g
Protein	1g
Vitamin C	8%
Vitamin A	1%
Iron	2%
Calcium	2%

Ingredients

- 6 green apples, peeled, cored and finely sliced
- 1/3 cup + ½ cup of raw sugar
- ¾ cup + 1 tablespoon of almond flour
- 1 tsp. of cinnamon
- ½ cup of coconut oil
- 2 tsps. of cinnamon

Method

- Preheat the oven to 350°F.

- Combine the apple, 1/3 cup of raw sugar, 1 tsp. of cinnamon and 1 tbsp. of almond flour in a large bowl and transfer to an oven-safe pan distributing it evenly on the bottom.
- In another bowl, mix the remaining ingredients and then combine them using your hands until the mixture acquires the texture of coarse sand grains.
- Cover the apple layer with this mixture and bake for 30 minutes or until golden.

Tip – A flavorful variation of this recipe consists in substituting apples for pears and adding a tbsp. of sweet wine such as Port to the fruit layer.

28. Fake Chocolate Truffles

Preparation time	30minutes
Ready time	30hour
Serves	20 truffles
Serving quantity/unit	1 truffle/ 40g / 1.5 ounces
Calories	209Cal
Total Fat	17g
Cholesterol	0mg
Sodium	11mg
Total Carbohydrates	13g
Dietary fibers	4g
Sugars	5g
Protein	5g
Vitamin C	0%
Vitamin A	0%
Iron	10%
Calcium	10%

Ingredients

- ½ pound of almond flour
- ½ pound of finely chopped almonds
- 1 cup of almond butter
- ½ cup of tahini
- ¾ cup of carob flour
- 4 tbsps. of dried, unsweetened coconut
- 3 tbsp. of raw honey
- 4 tbsps. of dried, unsweetened coconut to coat

Method

- Combine all the ingredients (except the coating coconut) in a mixing ball until homogeneous. Let sit for 15-20 minutes in the refrigerator.

- Scoop out small portions of dough and, using your hands, shape them into balls.
- Dip the balls in the remaining dried coconut to coat them.

Tip - you can buy almond butter in health food stores, or make it at home using a good quality food processor and grind it to an almond paste.

You can use raw cocoa powder instead of carob flour.

29. Spicy Chocolate Cake

Preparation time	30 minutes
Ready time	1 hour
Serves	8
Serving quantity/unit	106G / 4ounces
Calories	308Cal
Total Fat	25G
Cholesterol	82mg
Sodium	324mg
Total Carbohydrates	19g
Dietary fibers	2g
Sugars	16g
Protein	6g
Vitamin C	1%
Vitamin A	2%
Iron	6%
Calcium	5%

Ingredients

Cake

- 4 eggs, yolks and whites separated
- 1/3 cup of coconut oil, melted
- 1/3 cup of almond milk
- ¼ cup of raw honey
- 1 tsp. of pure vanilla extract
- 1 tbsp. of baking soda
- 3.5 oz. of unsweetened dark chocolate, melted
- 1 ½ tsps. of cinnamon
- 1 tsp. of ginger
- ½ tsp. cardamom
- ½ tsp. of cloves
- 1 ¾ cups of almond flour

Frosting

- 3 tbsps. of coconut oil, melted
- 2 tbsps. of raw honey
- 1 tsp. of cinnamon
- ¼ cup of almond flour
- ¼ cup of finely chopped almonds

Method

- Preheat the oven to 350ºF.
- Grease a cake pan with a tbsp. of coconut oil and line it with non-stick baking paper.
- Combine the yolks, the remaining oil, and honey in a large bowl and add the milk and vanilla extract.
- Mix flour with baking soda, chocolate and spices. Add to the yolk mixture.
- Beat the egg whites until stiff and carefully fold them in the cake batter.
- Pour the batter into the cake pan.
- Combine all the frosting ingredients in a mixing bowl and spread the mixture over the cake batter.
- Bake for 30 minutes or until a toothpick comes out clean.

Tip – To get new flavors out of this cake recipe, try adding lemon or orange zest to the cake batter or even ½ cup of pumpkin puree.

30. Peanut Cookies

Preparation time	30 minutes
Ready time	45 minutes
Serves	10 cookies
Serving quantity/unit	1 cookie/ 40g / 1.5 ounces
Calories	159Cal
Total Fat	12g
Cholesterol	0mg
Sodium	141mg
Total Carbohydrates	10g
Dietary fibers	2g
Sugars	8g
Protein	5g
Vitamin C	0%
Vitamin A	0%
Iron	4%
Calcium	2%

Ingredients

- ¾ cup peanut flour
- ¾ cup of almond flour
- 2 egg whites
- 4 tbsps. of raw honey
- 3 tbsps. of coconut oil, melted
- 1 tsp. of baking soda

Method

- Preheat the oven to 350°F.
- Combine all the ingredients in a mixing ball until homogeneous. Let sit for 15-20 minutes in the refrigerator.
- Scoop out small portions of dough and, shape them into balls. Press each ball with the palm of your hand to form a cookie shape.
- Bake for 10-15 minutes or until the edges are golden.

Tip – To prepare peanut flour, get unsalted, roasted peanuts, put them in a food processor and pulse to a fine powder.

31. Almond Biscuits

Preparation time	30 minutes
Ready time	1hour 30 minutes
Serves	10 biscuits
Serving quantity/unit	1 biscuit/ 40G / 1.5ounces
Calories	88Cal
Total Fat	5g
Cholesterol	33mg
Sodium	93mg
Total Carbohydrates	8g
Dietary fibers	1g
Sugars	6g
Protein	3g
Vitamin C	7%
Vitamin A	1%
Iron	3%
Calcium	3%

Ingredients

- ½ cup of chopped almonds

- 1 ½ cup of almond flour
- Zest of one orange
- 2 tsps. of pure vanilla essence
- 3 tbsps. of raw honey
- a pinch of salt
- 2 eggs
- ½ teaspoon of baking soda

Method

- Preheat the oven to 300ºF.
- Combine all the ingredients in a mixing ball until homogeneous. Let sit for 15-20 minutes.
- Roll the dough into 1inch diameter cylinders.
- Bake for 15-20 minutes.
- Remove from the oven, let cool. Cut diagonal slices.
- Set the oven temperature to 280F.
- Lay the biscuits in a baking tray lined with a baking sheet. Bake them for 30-35 minutes.

Tip – Instead of chopped almonds you can use walnuts and add finely chopped dried fruits such as apricot to the dough to create different types of biscuits.

32. Coffee and Vanilla Delights

Preparation time	30minutes
Ready time	30 minutes
Serves	8 small units
Serving quantity/unit	30g / 1 ounce
Calories	60Cal
Total Fat	5g
Cholesterol	0mg
Sodium	2mg
Total Carbohydrates	5g
Dietary fibers	1g
Sugars	4g
Protein	1g
Vitamin C	0%
Vitamin A	0%
Iron	2%
Calcium	1%

Ingredients

- 1 cup of almond flour

- 1 tbsp. of coconut oil
- 1 ½ tbsp. of coffee (or 1 tsp. of instant coffee dissolved in 1 tbsp. of warm water)
- 1 tsp. of vanilla essence
- 2 tbsps. of coconut milk
- 2 tbsps. of raw sugar
- Unsweetened cocoa powder

Method

- Combine all the ingredients (except the cocoa powder) in a mixing ball until homogeneous. Let sit for 15-20 minutes in the refrigerator.
- Scoop out small portions of dough and shape them into balls using your hands.
- Dip the balls in the coconut powder to coat them.

Tip – Instead of using cocoa powder to coat the balls, try using some dried, unsweetened shredded coconut or other dried fruit finely chopped, crushed nuts or your favorite seeds.

33. Crust-less Fresh Plum Pie

Preparation time	30 minutes
Ready time	1 hour
Serves	8
Serving quantity/unit	174g / 6 ounces
Calories	308Cal
Total Fat	18g
Cholesterol	82mg
Sodium	33mg
Total Carbohydrates	36g
Dietary fibers	2g
Sugars	33g
Protein	4g
Vitamin C	16%
Vitamin A	9%
Iron	4%
Calcium	3%

Ingredients

- ½ cup of coconut oil, melted
- ¾ cup of raw sugar
- 2 tbsps. of raw honey
- 4 eggs
- 1 ¼ cup of almond flour

- 12 fresh plums, halved and pitted

Method

- Pre-heat oven to 350F.
- Combine eggs, oil, honey and sugar in a mixing ball.
- Stir in almond flour.
- Transfer the plum halves to an oven safe pan (cut side down).
- Pour over the almond flour mixture.
- Bake for 20-35 minutes or until golden.

Tip – Instead of using plums, you can also use fresh apricots, raspberries or blueberries for a dessert with a completely different look and taste.

34. Dried Apricot and Strawberry Cake

Preparation time	30 minutes
Ready time	1hour
Serves	8
Serving quantity/unit	106g / 4ounces
Calories	256Cal
Total Fat	17g
Cholesterol	41mg
Sodium	177mg
Total Carbohydrates	22g
Dietary fibers	4g
Sugars	16g
Protein	7g
Vitamin C	25%
Vitamin A	11%
Iron	8%
Calcium	8%

Ingredients

- 2 cups of almond meal
- 1 tbsp. of flaxseed meal
- 1 cup of strawberries, chopped
- 6 dried apricots
- 1/3 cup of almond milk
- 1 + 1 tbsp. of coconut oil
- 1/3 cup of raw honey
- 2 eggs, yolks and whites separated

- 1 teaspoon of baking soda

Method

- Preheat the oven to 350°F.
- Grease a cake pan with a tbsp. of coconut oil and line it with non-stick baking paper.
- Combine the yolks, the remaining oil, and honey in a large bowl and add the milk.
- Mix flour with baking soda, and flaxseed meal. Add to the yolk mixture.
- Puree the strawberries and apricots in a food processor. Add to the cake batter.
- Beat the egg whites until stiff and carefully fold them in the batter.
- Pour the batter into the cake pan.
- Bake for 30 minutes or until a toothpick comes out clean.

Tip – For additional flavor, spread your favorite frosting over the cake after it has cooled down. Half a cup of coconut milk, simmered with a couple tablespoons of raw cocoa makes for a tasty option.

35. Pancakes

Preparation time	10 minutes
Ready time	20 minutes
Serves	2 large pancakes
Serving quantity/unit	1 pancake/278g/10ounces
Calories	552Cal
Total Fat	50g
Cholesterol	164mg
Sodium	86mg
Total Carbohydrates	16g
Dietary fibers	7g
Sugars	5g
Protein	18g
Vitamin C	1%
Vitamin A	4%
Iron	19%
Calcium	20%

Ingredients

- 2 eggs
- 2 tbsps. of coconut oil
- 2 tbsps. of almond milk
- 1 tsp. of raw sugar
- 4 tbsps. of almond flour

- ½ tbsp. of flaxseed meal
- ½ teaspoon baking powder

Method

- Combine all the ingredients in a food processor until smooth.
- Heat a skillet over medium heat.
- Pour in one scoop of batter and cook for 2-3 minutes on each side or until golden.
- Repeat the process until you've used all the batter.

Tip – Combine 2 tbsps. of raw honey with a tbsp. of lemon juice to make your own pancake syrup. For a vitamin boost, serve the pancakes with fresh fruits such as strawberries, small pieces of cantaloupe melon or mango slices.

36. Fig and Almond Ice Cream

Preparation time	30 minutes
Ready time	5hours
Serves	10
Serving quantity/unit	230g / 8ounces
Calories	293Cal
Total Fat	15g
Cholesterol	0mg
Sodium	10mg
Total Carbohydrates	39g
Dietary fibers	6g
Sugars	20g
Protein	3g
Vitamin C	9%
Vitamin A	4%
Iron	8%
Calcium	8%

Ingredients

- 1 cup of almond flour
- 2 tbsps. of flaxseed meal
- 2 1/4 cups of almond milk
- 10 figs, chopped
- ½ tbsp. of lemon zest
- 1/2 cup of water
- 1/4 cup of raw honey

Method

- Combine the figs, lemon zest, honey and water in a saucepan and bring to a simmer.
- Simmer for 10-15 minutes or until the figs are soft and the syrup thickens. Remove from heat. Let cool.
- Combine the remaining ingredients in a mixing bowl.
- Stir in the fig mixture.
- Put in the freezer and stir it every 1 or 2 hours to improve the ice cream texture.

Tip – Instead of fresh figs, you can use the same quantity of dried figs and hydrate them in a mixture of water and Port wine for 1 hour, before simmering.

37. Baked Pears with Almond Crust

Preparation time	30minutes
Ready time	1hour
Serves	10
Serving quantity/unit	146g / 5 ounces
Calories	218Cal
Total Fat	13G
Cholesterol	65mg
Sodium	30mg
Total Carbohydrates	25G
Dietary fibers	4G
Sugars	19G
Protein	4G
Vitamin C	7%
Vitamin A	2%
Iron	6%
Calcium	4%

Ingredients

- ¼ cup of almond flour
- 1 cup of almond milk
- 4 eggs
- ½ cup of chopped almonds
- 4 pears, peeled, cored and halved
- 2 tbsps. of coconut oil, melted
- 1/3 cup of raw honey

Method

- Pre-heat the oven to 300F.
- Combine all the ingredients (except pears) in a mixing bowl.
- Put the pears in an oven safe dish (cut side down).
- Pour over the almond mixture.
- Bake for 30 minutes or until golden.

Tip – Add a couple drops of pure vanilla essence to the almond mixture to get different layers of flavor. You can also use peaches instead of pears.

38. Almond Meringues

Preparation time	20 minutes
Ready time	50minutes
Serves	15 meringues
Serving quantity/unit	1 meringue/32g/1ounce
Calories	57Cal
Total Fat	1g
Cholesterol	0mg
Sodium	26mg
Total Carbohydrates	11g
Dietary fibers	0g
Sugars	10g
Protein	2g
Vitamin C	0%
Vitamin A	0%
Iron	0%
Calcium	1%

Ingredients

- 1 cup of almond flour
- ¾ cup of raw sugar
- 7 egg whites

Method

- Pre-heat oven to 250F.
- Line a baking sheet with parchment paper.
- Combine almond flour and sugar in a food processor to form a finer powder.
- Beat the egg whites until stiff. Slowly fold in almond and sugar.
- Use a pastry bag to put small portions of meringue onto the baking sheet.

- Bake for 20 to 30 minutes.

Tip – For a whole new flavor, add a few drops of almond or vanilla essence, lemon zest or a couple teaspoons of cocoa powder to the mixture.

39. Panforte

Preparation time	30minutes
Ready time	1hour
Serves	6
Serving quantity/unit	130G / 5 ounces
Calories	483Cal
Total Fat	29g
Cholesterol	0mg
Sodium	8mg
Total Carbohydrates	58g
Dietary fibers	9g
Sugars	44g
Protein	10g
Vitamin C	4%
Vitamin A	3%
Iron	25%
Calcium	12%

Ingredients

- 3.5 oz. of almonds
- 3.5 oz. of hazelnuts
- ¼ cup of raw palm sugar
- 1/3 cup of dried figs, chopped
- 1/3 cup of apricots, chopped
- 1/3 cup of white raisins
- ¾ cup of almond flour
- 1 tbsp. flaxseed meal softened in 2 tbsps. of warm water
- 2 tbsps. of unsweetened cocoa powder
- 1 tsp. of ground cinnamon
- ½ tsp. of nutmeg
- ½ cup of honey
- 2.5 oz. of unsweetened chocolate, chopped
- 1 tbsp. of coconut oil, melted

Method

- Preheat the oven to 350°F.
- Grease an oven safe round pan with coconut oil and line it with parchment paper.
- Place the almonds and hazelnuts in a large bowl. Add flaxseed, figs, apricots and raisins, mix.
- Sift over the flour, cocoa, cinnamon and nutmeg, mix.
- Place the chocolate, honey and sugar in a small saucepan over low heat until the sugar dissolves and the chocolate melts.
- Bring to a simmer, and let cook for 2 minutes.
- Pour the hot chocolate mixture over the fruit and, carefully, mix until homogeneous.
- Pour into the previously prepared pan.
- Bake for 30-35 minutes.

Tip – You can make innumerous variations of this dessert using different dried fruits and adding the zest of a citrus fruit like orange to the batter.

40. Banana Muffins

Preparation time	30minutes
Ready time	50 minutes
Serves	6muffins
Serving quantity/unit	1 muffin/ 80g / 3ounces
Calories	144Cal
Total Fat	8G
Cholesterol	55mg
Sodium	24mg
Total Carbohydrates	18g
Dietary fibers	2g
Sugars	11g
Protein	3g
Vitamin C	6%
Vitamin A	2%
Iron	4%
Calcium	13%

Ingredients

- 2 bananas, mashed
- 3 tbsps. of raw palm sugar
- 1 tbsp. of flaxseed meal softened in 1 tbsp. of warm water
- ½ cup of almond flour
- 2 eggs, yolks and whites separated
- 2 tbsps. of coconut oil, melted

- 1 tbsp. of baking powder
- 1 tsp. of vanilla essence
- 1 ½ tsp. of cinnamon

Method

- Preheat the oven to 350F.
- Combine the yolks, flaxseed, oil, and sugar in a large bowl. Add the banana, vanilla and cinnamon and stir.
- Mix flour with baking soda and add to the egg mixture.
- Beat the egg whites until stiff and carefully fold them in the cake batter.
- Pour the batter into 6 muffin paper liners, and bake for 20-25 minutes or until muffins are light golden brown and a toothpick comes out clean.

Tip – Instead of mashed bananas, you can also use pureed apple or pear, or even cooked and mashed carrots or pumpkin.

41. Nuts and Dates No-Bake Brownie

Preparation time	30minutes
Ready time	1hour
Serves	8
Serving quantity/unit	110g / 4ounces
Calories	322Cal
Total Fat	15G
Cholesterol	0mg
Sodium	80mg
Total Carbohydrates	51g
Dietary fibers	10g
Sugars	36g
Protein	9g
Vitamin C	1%
Vitamin A	0%
Iron	16%
Calcium	6%

Ingredients

- 1 cup of walnuts, chopped
- 2 ½ cups of dried dates, chopped
- 1 cup of unsweetened cocoa powder
- 2 cups of almond flour
- 1 tbsp. of flax seed softened in 2 tbsps. of water

- ¼ teaspoon of salt

Method

- Combine all the ingredients (except walnuts) in a food processor and pulse until homogeneous.
- If the mixture is too dry, add a couple more dates.
- Combine the mixture with the nuts in a mixing bowl.
- Transfer to a rectangular and refrigerate overnight.
- Remove from the refrigerator 15-20 minutes before serving

Tip – After refrigerating, cut into individual portions and take one with you to work for a quick and energizing snack.

42. Almond Mousse

Preparation time	20minutes
Ready time	1 hour
Serves	8
Serving quantity/unit	115g / 4 ounces
Calories	214Cal
Total Fat	11G
Cholesterol	143mg
Sodium	59mg
Total Carbohydrates	23g
Dietary fibers	2g
Sugars	20g
Protein	8g
Vitamin C	3%
Vitamin A	4%
Iron	7%
Calcium	6%

Ingredients

- ¾ cup of raw palm sugar
- ¼ cup of water
- Zest of one lemon
- 7 eggs, yolks and whites separated
- 1 tablespoon of cinnamon
- 3.5 oz. of almond flour
- 3 tbsps. of almonds, chopped

Method

- Put sugar in a saucepan, add the water and lemon zest and bring to a simmer over low heat for about 5 minutes. Remove from heat.
- In a mixing bowl, combine egg yolks, cinnamon and almond flour. Add the sugar syrup stirring continuously.
- Transfer the mixture to a saucepan and heat it over medium heat. Let cook, stirring for 3-4 minutes so it thickens a little. Remove from heat and let cool.
- Heat a skillet over medium heat, add the chopped almonds and toast them for 3-4 minutes.
- Beat the egg whites until stiff fold in the yolk mixture. Transfer to a serving dish, and refrigerate.
- Serve with the toasted almonds on top

Tip – Also, with this dish, there are several variations possible. Just by adding cocoa powder and a pinch of red pepper (instead of cinnamon), you'll have a totally different dessert.

43. Crusted Apple Pie

Preparation time	30minutes
Ready time	1hour 30 minutes
Serves	8
Serving quantity/unit	116g / 4 ounces
Calories	288Cal
Total Fat	22g
Cholesterol	41mg
Sodium	93mg
Total Carbohydrates	21g
Dietary fibers	4g
Sugars	16g
Protein	5g
Vitamin C	4%
Vitamin A	2%
Iron	5%
Calcium	5%

Ingredients

Crust

- 2 cups of almond flour
- 3 tbsps. of coconut oil, melted
- 1 egg
- ¼ tsp. of salt

Filling

- 2/3 cup of almonds
- 1 tbsp. of flaxseed meal
- 4 tbsps. of raw palm sugar
- 2 tbsps. of raw honey
- 5 tbsps. of coconut oil, melted
- 1 egg
- 2 apples, peeled, cored, finely sliced
- 2 tsps. of cinnamon

Method

- Pre-heat oven to 350F.
- Line a pie pan with non-stick baking paper.
- To make the crust, combine the almond flour with coconut oil, egg and salt.
- Put it in the pie pan. Shape it covering the bottom and sides of the pan.
- Bake for about 20 minutes or until light golden.
- Combine apple, cinnamon and 1 tbsp. of sugar in a mixing bowl. Set aside.
- To make the filling, combine all the remaining ingredients (except the apple and cinnamon) in a bowl and stir until smooth.
- Cover the bottom of the crust with the apple slices. Pour over the filling mixture. Bake for 25-30 minutes.

Tip – If you're trying to cut back on the calories but are still craving for something sweet, make this pie without the crust. You'll have full flavor for a lot less calories.

44. Raspberry and Blueberry Bars

Preparation time	30minutes
Ready time	1hour
Serves	10
Serving quantity/unit	107G / 4 ounces
Calories	372Cal
Total Fat	30g
Cholesterol	16mg
Sodium	10mg
Total Carbohydrates	27g
Dietary fibers	3g
Sugars	23g
Protein	4g
Vitamin C	9%
Vitamin A	1%
Iron	5%
Calcium	3%

Ingredients

- 2 cups of almond flour
- 1 cup of hazelnuts
- 1 egg, whisked
- 2 tbsps. of flaxseed meal softened in 4 tbsps. of water
- 1 cup of coconut oil, melted
- 3/4 cup of raw honey
- 1 cup of raspberries
- 1 cup of blueberries

Method

- Preheat the oven to 350F.
- Line a square pan with parchment paper.
- Combine the almond flour and hazelnuts in a food processor and pulse to a fine powder.
- Transfer to a mixing bowl. Add the coconut oil, honey, egg and mix using your hands, you should end up with a crumbly consistency.
- Use 2/3 of the dough to line the pan.
- Add the fruits.
- Cover with the remaining dough.
- Bake for 35 minutes or until golden.
- Remove and let cool before cutting it.

Tip – For a creamier filling, add a couple tablespoons of whole coconut milk.

If you can't find fresh raspberries and blueberries, the frozen versions or finely chopped strawberries make for great alternatives.

45. Chocolate and Coconut Biscuits

Preparation time	20 minutes
Ready time	40 minutes
Serves	12 biscuits
Serving quantity/unit	1 biscuit/ 54g / 2ounces
Calories	143Cal
Total Fat	7
Cholesterol	0mg
Sodium	22mg
Total Carbohydrates	20
Dietary fibers	2g
Sugars	17g
Protein	3g
Vitamin C	1%
Vitamin A	0%
Iron	11%
Calcium	1%

Ingredients

- 1 2/3 cup of almond flour
- 4 egg whites
- 1 cup sugar
- ½ cup of unsweetened chocolate, melted
- 1 cup of shredded, unsweetened coconut

Method

- Preheat the oven to 350°F.
- Line a baking tray with parchment paper.
- Beat the egg whites until stiff.
- Carefully fold in the almond flour, then the coconut and, finally, the chocolate.
- Scoop small portions of cookie batter onto the baking tray and bake for 20 minutes.

Tip – For a crunchier texture, add some chopped nuts to the batter.

46. Almond and Flaxseed Muffins

Preparation time	30minutes
Ready time	1hour
Serves	10 muffins
Serving quantity/unit	1 muffin/80g / 3 ounces
Calories	250Cal
Total Fat	19g
Cholesterol	65mg
Sodium	148mg
Total Carbohydrates	12
Dietary fibers	7g
Sugars	10g
Protein	7g
Vitamin C	0%
Vitamin A	2%
Iron	8%
Calcium	12%

Ingredients

- 1 cup of flaxseed
- 1 cup of almond flour
- 1 tbsp. of baking powder
- ½ tsp. of salt
- 1 tsp. of nutmeg
- 1 tsp. of cinnamon
- ½ cup of raw palm sugar
- ½ cup of coconut oil, melted
- 4 eggs, yolks and whites separated
- ½ cup water

Method

- Preheat the oven to 350°F.
- Combine the yolks, oil and sugar in a large bowl. Stir in the water.
- Combine the almond flour and flaxseeds in a food processor and pulse to a fine powder.
- Transfer to a mixing bowl, add the spices, salt and baking powder. Add to the egg mixture.
- Beat the egg whites until stiff and carefully fold them in the cake batter.
- Pour the batter into 10 muffin paper liners and bake for 20 minutes or until golden.

Tip – If you're looking for a crunchier texture, you can add some chopped walnuts to the cake batter.

47. Orange and Apricot Muffins

Preparation time	30minutes
Ready time	1hour
Serves	6 muffins
Serving quantity/unit	1muffin/ 76g / 2.5 ounces
Calories	217Cal
Total Fat	15g
Cholesterol	109mg
Sodium	44mg
Total Carbohydrates	18g
Dietary fibers	1g
Sugars	17g
Protein	5g
Vitamin C	4%
Vitamin A	4%
Iron	9%
Calcium	2%

Ingredients

- 4 eggs, yolks and whites separated
- 1/3 cup of raw honey
- ¼ cup of coconut oil, melted
- ½ cup of dried, unsweetened coconut (grated)
- ½ cup of almond flour
- 2 tbsps. of finely chopped dried apricot
- 1 tbsp. of orange zest

Method

- Preheat the oven to 350°F.
- Combine the yolks, oil and honey in a mixing bowl.
- Combine the almond flour with the grated coconut. Add to the yolk mixture
- Stir in the orange zest and apricot.
- Beat the egg whites until stiff and carefully fold them in the cake batter.
- Pour the batter into 6 muffin paper liners and bake for 20 minutes or until golden.

Tip – If you like to use dried fruit in your recipes, you'll find there are innumerous variations to this recipe. Try replacing the dried apricot with dried cherries, prunes, raisins or mango.

Books by Donatella Giordano

Coconut Flour! 47+ Irresistible Recipes for Baking with Coconut Flour

Almond Flour! Gluten Free & Paleo Diet Cookbook

www.amazon.com/author/donatellagiordano

About Donatella Giordano

In addition to being an acclaimed chef, Donatella Giordano is considered an expert in the field of gourmet, gluten-free and paleo cooking.

Through her tasty natural gluten-free recipes, she has gradually managed to win over her husband, three kids and two chocolate labradors, all of whom now love their healthy diets and lifestyles.

Exclusive Bonus Download: Coconut Oil - The Healthy Fat

Download your bonus, please visit the download link above from your PC or MAC. To open PDF files, visit http://get.adobe.com/reader/ to download the reader if it's not already installed on your PC or Mac. To open ZIP files, you may need to download WinZip from http://www.winzip.com. This download is for PC or Mac ONLY and might not be downloadable to kindle.

Coconut oil the complete natural health guide!

Find out the health benefits of coconut oil today!

Find out how coconut oil can, cure common illnesses saving you hundreds in doctors' fees, help you lose weight without losing the great taste of your favorite foods and much, much more!

Coconut oil has long been held in high repute by natural health specialists and doctors from a massively diverse range of countries. Western medicine has been slow to catch on to the health benefits of coconut oil but cutting edge research is finally catching up to what eastern doctors have known for centuries; COCONUT OIL IS GOOD FOR YOU!

Whilst many claims are made about the benefits of coconut oil in your diet and as a topical skin treatment finding good information on the wide range of benefits coconut oil can have for you can be incredibly time consuming and tricky.

Get the Facts about coconut oil health today!

This eBook has been compiled for exactly these reasons we have spent weeks crawling cyberspace and reading medical reports to try and find as much concrete information on the myriad of benefits that coconut oil can offer YOU. This guide gives you a complete breakdown of all the health benefits of coconut oil and a complete guide to how YOU can start using it to improve your health.

This book tells you when to use coconut oil, why you should be using coconut oil and how coconut oil can improve your health AND cure common illnesses

Our complete guide to natural coconut oil health gives you a comprehensive insight into:

- Coconut oil and your hair – Find out whether coconut oil can improve the condition of your hair. Plus a comprehensive exposition of whether coconut oil can prevent hair loss and re-invigorate your hair.
- Coconut oil and skincare – Find out how coconut oil can keep your skin looking young fresh and firm. Plus find out which skin afflictions and disease you can cure just with coconut oil!
- Coconut oil and weight loss – Find out why coconut oil is a surprisingly effective aid to weight loss and how best to get it into your diet. Learn how you can utilize coconut oil and start shedding pounds now!
- Coconut oil and digestion – Find out how coconut oil can cure indigestion, how coconut oils help your digestive system stay healthy and why coconut oil increases your metabolism.

- Coconut oil and your immune system – Find out how coconut oil can drastically improve your immune system as part of a well-balanced diet.
- Can coconut oil help fight infections? – Find out about the huge number of infections simple, natural coconut oil can fight and how it can prevent common illnesses.
- And finally
- Coconut oil and heart disease – Find out the truth about one of the most controversial claims being made NOW about coconut oil. We examine the evidence in depth and see what the benefits are of coconut oil for a healthy heart.

This book covers everything you could ever need to know about coconut oil and will save you hundreds of dollars on expensive medicines and beauty products.

Knowing the secrets we reveal in this book will improve your health and will be an important step in helping you to live a long and fruitful life. Happy health!

Visit the URL above to download this guide and start overall health and weight loss goals NOW

One Last Thing...

Thank you so much for reading my book. I hope you really liked it. As you probably know, many people look at the reviews on Amazon before they decide to purchase a book. If you liked the book, could you please take a minute to leave a review with your feedback? 60 seconds is all I'm asking for, and it would mean the world to me.

******

Donatella Giordano

Copyright © 2012 Donatella Giordano

Images and Cover by NaturalWay Publishing

Atlanta, Georgia USA

Made in the USA
Lexington, KY
04 January 2015